W9-AVK-765

ACHIEVING FLUENCY
in ENGLISH

A Text for ESL and Basic Writers

Fourth Edition

Adele MacGowan-Gilhooly
City College of the
City University of New York

KENDALL/HUNT PUBLISHING COMPANY
4050 Westmark Drive   Dubuque, Iowa 52002

What we learn with pleasure,
we never forget.

–Alfred Mercier

Contents

Preface to the Teacher vii

Acknowledgments ix

Chapter One: How to Achieve Fluent Writing & Reading   1

Chapter Two: Learning with Others   7

Chapter Three: Reading Novels to Develop Fluency   9

Chapter Four: Free Writing to Develop Fluency   17

Chapter Five: Writing Non-Fiction to Develop Fluency   23

Chapter Six: Developing the Craft of Writing   33

Chapter Seven: Writing Our Lives to Develop Fluency   43

Chapter Eight: Describing People, Places & Actions   57

Chapter Nine: Point-of-View Writing to Develop Fluency   65

Chapter Ten: Writing Your "Novelette" or Short Stories   69

Chapter Eleven: Dialogues, Monologues, & Other
                    Composing Techniques   81

Chapter Twelve: Revising   85

Chapter Thirteen: Editing   95

Chapter Fourteen: More Editing for Verb Errors 109

Chapter Fifteen: Publishing Your Work 119

Bibliography 123

Preface to the Teacher

The purpose of this book is to help students learn to write and to read fluently in English. This means that they will learn to read extensively with good comprehension, and to write comprehensible, complete and logical pieces with comfort and control. *Achieving Fluency* can be used over one semester or two. I wrote it with college ESL students in mind, but it can also be used with any basic writers, including native speakers of English, high school, middle school and adult education students. Anyone who has not yet developed fluency in writing and/or reading, and therefore is finding academic reading and writing difficult, will benefit from the approach and activities herein. The book is not for beginning ESL students.

The book asks students to write a 10,000-word "book" or "books," do daily free writing, read 1,000 pages of fiction, respond in journals, and work in small groups to better understand their readings and to improve their written pieces. Students also learn to write expressive, narrative, and descriptive pieces. They learn to revise their own writing and to help others revise theirs. And they learn to bring their own questions and knowledge to what they are reading, as well as to develop their knowledge of vocabulary, syntax, spelling, and of how written English flows, all on a highly individualized basis. All this exposure to English also augments their knowledge of the mechanics of written English.

The "book" students are asked to write can be an autobiography, a fictional autobiography, a collection of stories, a novelette, an historical novelette, or a magazine. The massive English writing, reading and interaction afforded by this approach improves students' oral skills. But above all, it dramatically augments and accelerates their reading and writing development, because it immerses them in extensive, pleasurable literacy activities, and postpones the need to monitor for correctness until they are fluent. Yet in the process, they tend to become more and more correct. Achieving Fluency is not just about writing; it also offers a rich reading experience, with many examples of writing, new vocabulary and exposure to various genres.

The second book in this series, *Achieving Clarity in English,* helps students to bridge over to academic writing, and the third book, *Achieving Correctness in Academic Writing,* helps them to write academic essays in correct English. Accompanying the books is a teacher reference book, *Fluency First: A Guide for Teachers,* with chapters on the theoretical bases for this whole-language approach, the Fluency First curriculum, writing samples, assessment ideas, and a list of books with movies that work well with this approach.

Some that have been used successfully at the fluency level are *Flowers for Algernon, The Karate Kid, Fly Away Home, The Wizard of Oz, The Outsiders, Jaws, Diary of Anne Frank, Uncle Tom's Cabin, Charlotee's Web, Rebecca, 'Till We Meet Again, The Rescuer, Nights in Rodanthe, The Guardian, Cry the Beloved Country, Their Eyes Were Watching God, Black Like Me,* and many more. Reading the novel and seeing the movie both promote acquisition of the language in general, and of fluency in English reading. If some of these books are too difficult for your students, you can start with simplified versions of books with movies like *20,000 Leagues Under the Sea.*

Both students and teachers have enjoyed the Fluency First approach at CCNY and other schools; I'm sure you and your students will, too.

Acknowledgments

I owe considerable thanks to my colleague at the City College of New York, Dr. Barbara Gleason, director of the M.A. Program in Language and Literacy, for her extensive review and critique of this book. I also wish to thank my CCNY colleague, Dr. Elizabeth Rorschach, who co-directs the Fluency First Project with me, and Anthea Tillyer, founder of the TESL-L email network, for the many practical things I have learned from them about the teaching of writing. Many thanks and compliments are due, too, to the Fluency First teachers and students in the former ESL department at the City College of New York. The teachers' enthusiasm for the Fluency First approach over several years made our classes exciting and successful beyond our expectations; and the students' work at creating wonderful books and magazines has taught us a great deal about language learning.

To help Fluency First students achieve fluency in writing, we ask them to write expressively and to tell their stories. Thus, in writing this book for them, I consulted four sources. The first two, published by the Teachers and Writers Collaborative, are Karen M. Hubert's book, *Teaching and Writing Popular Fiction: Horror, Adventure, Mystery and Romance;* and Meredith Sue Willis' book, *Personal Fiction Writing: A guide to writing from real life.* The other two, published by Heinemann, are Creating the Story by Rebecca Rule and Susan Wheeler; and Turning Memories into Memoirs by Denis Ledoux. I am also indebted to Nancie Atwell for her many ideas on literacy materials, organization, activities, assessment and theory in her book, my favorite resource, *In the Middle,* also published by Heinemann.

Over the past several years, my colleagues and I at CCNY have trained several hundred teachers around the country in the Fluency First approach, and during those workshops I have gotten many useful ideas for activities, books and movies from those talented teachers. Several of those ideas are in this book, but I cannot say whose they are since it is difficult to remember where one gets good ideas when one gets so many. I'll just say, "Thank you for all of your help with this book." Those colleagues include faculty from Essex, Union, and Atlantic Cape Community Colleges (NJ), Broward Community College (FL), Salem State and Middlesex Community Colleges (MA), LaGuardia, Bronx and Queensborough Community Colleges (NYC), Harrisburg Area Community College (PA), Monroe Community College (NY), NOVA Community College (VA), University of Oregon at Eugene, and UNC Charlotte.

Finally, I wish to thank my husband, Ed, and my daughter, Natasha, for their contributions to this book.

Chapter One

HOW TO ACHIEVE FLUENT WRITING & READING

Do you read and write fluently? That is, do you read at a normal pace and understand most of what you read without relying on a dictionary? Do you write with comfort, control and automaticity, and use writing to express yourself, to report things, to tell stories, to discover ideas, to think, and to learn? If not, this book is for you. But first, let me tell you a nice story.

Some years ago, large numbers of our ESL students at CCNY were not fluent readers or writers, and they were not getting much better by just studying grammar, reading sample essays and writing essays. The reason? They lacked fluency. To achieve fluency in writing and reading, you have to do a lot of both, but those students had not done much of either. So began the Fluency First project. Our ESL students now had to read novels and write a 10,000-word "book" in each writing course. This gave them so much exposure to English that their writing, reading and test scores on the college writing and reading tests more than doubled. And ESL course repetition rates were cut in half. This book will help you to learn just as much as they did.

Up to now, you may not have read much, either. And maybe you have never done the kinds and amounts of writing needed to become fluent. Perhaps you even avoid writing. Yet to become fluent in writing, you must write a lot, stop worrying about errors, and concentrate on expressing your ideas the best you can. Just as you made mistakes learning to speak when you were a child, you will make mistakes in writing. It's normal, and it helps you to learn.

Similarly, when you are beginning to read a book, you may meet new words that you do not understand. But if you tolerate this confusion and keep reading, you will probably figure out most of the words, and even more important, you will enjoy reading much more. By the time you finish the book, you will have become a more fluent, proficient reader and writer.

In this book I ask you to read a few novels. That may seem like a lot, but you need to read only ten pages a day to keep up. After so much reading, you will be a much better reader, you will write better, and you will have a larger vocabulary. Best of all, you will really enjoy the novels once you get going. I also ask you to write a "book" or "books" totaling 10,000 words. That, too, may seem like a lot, but it amounts to just three or four pages a week. It is a total of 50 double-spaced, typed pages. You should write a collection of life stories, a magazine, and a novelette to reach 10,000 words.

In class, you will work with your classmates to try to improve your writing and theirs, and to discuss the books you read. Class will be like a workshop where you get together with others and work hard at the craft of writing, and to understand more of what you read than you likely would going solo.

In summary, as you work in the "Fluency First" approach, your reading and writing skills will improve in ways similar to how you learned to speak your first language: through abundant, enjoyable, important, meaning-driven practice. But I'm sure you have some questions. So I've taken the liberty to guess a few of them and respond.

What Will Classes Be Like?

In class, you will spend a good deal of your time writing and discussing that writing, your peers' writing, and the books you are reading. You will share your written pieces with peers and get their reactions. This will help you to hear your pieces as others hear them. You will then revise your written pieces, if needed, to improve them, keeping others' responses in mind. And as mentioned before, you will also be discussing the novels you are reading.

Your class will not be a traditional teacher-centered class with students progressing through the same material at the same pace. It will be highly individualized. You will ask your own questions, decide on your own writing topics, and respond as you see fit to reading.

Will I Learn Grammar?

Everyone worries about being correct, so naturally they believe that a grammar course will lead to correctness. This is not a grammar course, where correctness is the main concern, but one in which you must strive for fluency by making and negotiating meaning. Nonetheless, you **will learn a great deal of grammar,** as much or more than you would in a grammar course, as you read a thousand pages of popular fiction, containing tens of thousands of grammatically correct sentences and well developed paragraphs. You will read no misspelled words, and everything you read will be correctly punctuated. Through all this reading, you will develop a strong sense of syntax and spelling, and an extensive vocabulary.

Similarly, as you work to produce the amount and kinds of writing that are suggested in this text, you will learn even more grammar by experimenting with the language, and by asking teachers and peers for help when needed.

Once your writing is fluent, you will review the past and present verb tenses, word order, word forms, pronouns, spelling, and basic punctuation, since these will come up a lot during your writing this semester. And you will edit your fluent pieces for errors in those categories. But fluency is the priority, and I will explain why.

You best learn to read and write as you learned to speak: communicating about real ideas through massive doses of writing and reading, asking your own questions and expressing your own ideas, without worrying about correctness until you have achieved fluency, just as children do not worry about correctness as they learn to speak, but eventually, and effortlessly, without grammar lessons, they become fluent and then correct speakers. Similarly, composing first and editing later will help you to do both better.

Your teacher will help you with grammar and the mechanics of writing whenever you have a question, and when your writing becomes fluent and you are ready to edit. But don't worry about editing or correctness now. Focus on **the more important task in writing—composing.** If you are not sure of a spelling or verb ending, try it anyway; if you don't have all the word(s) for what you want to say, use the ones you do have; if you feel creative, express that creativity. These are ways to improve your writing.

What will I have for homework?

You will read your novels at home, and respond to them by writing in a double-entry journal; this will prepare you for class discussions. In your journal, you will comment and ask questions, rather than answer the teacher's questions. So you will enjoy reading the novel, yet be critical of it, as you might enjoy discussing and critiquing a movie or play you have seen.

What materials will I need?

1. two pocket folders (one for project pieces; one for journals)

2. plenty of loose leaf paper

3. a writer's notebook for free writing and other writing

4. erasable pens if you wish (but NO White-out)

5. transparent tape and scissors (or a computer & disks for word processing)

6. a highlighter

7. the paperback novels you will be reading

Conclusion

Have you ever sat in a class or done homework that was either too easy (boring) or too hard (frustrating)? If so, you surely wasted a lot of precious time. In this course, you will not waste time because you will learn what you need to learn, ask your own questions, and proceed at your own pace. At first, you may feel overburdened by how much work is expected of you. However, after a few weeks, you will read and write much faster, because you will have started to develop fluency in both. As a result, you will also enjoy both reading and writing much more. So what do you think of this approach?

Chapter Two

LEARNING WITH OTHERS

To understand the novels you are reading as well as academic reading, it is very helpful if you talk your way through the material with other students: asking your own questions, trying to explain things in your own words, and quizzing each other on what you are learning. These activities help you to remember more.

Likewise, to improve your writing, you should read it to others, find out what they think, then revise (make changes to improve it) as needed. In working with others like this, you will help each other to learn. But first, since many people are shy, we'll do a few things to break the ice.

Icebreaker Activity #1

If you haven't yet met a friend in class, you will today. First, write a list of questions you will ask your new friend, then introduce yourself to the person next to you. Interview that person and find out as many interesting, memorable things about them as possible. Take notes so that you will remember as much as possible. Then let the person interview you.

When you are finished, the teacher will put all the students in a big circle and you will each introduce the person you interviewed and tell what you have learned about them. As each student speaks, take notes on what s/he says. Try to remember as much as possible about each student, especially their names, and one or two interesting things about them. As others are introduced, jot down their names and try to remember them.

Icebreaker Activity #2

Sit with a group of 4 or 5 in a circle, and introduce yourselves again. One student will be the group leader, and the rest of you will be characters in the book you are reading, or even real-life characters. Discuss what's going on in the book or in your real-life character's life, and tell how you feel about it as that character. Ask others questions about their lives as well. Have fun, too.

Icebreaker Activity #3

With a group of four or five, read a few pages of the novel assigned by your teacher. The student with the best accent should read it aloud while the rest follow along. Stop whenever anyone has a question or a comment. You will be amazed at how much you learn. Then plan to meet for lunch or at the library to do the next reading assignment. When you meet, do the same. Try to set up a regular meeting time for your group to read, write and study together.

Icebreaker Activity #4

With your group, discuss and draw up some guidelines you should adhere to as you work together, whether discussing readings or listening to and making observations about each others' writing. Then write these up and have a group member report them to the class. The teacher will write the rules on the board, and the class will discuss them and decide on what will be the class rules during writing workshop and reading group discussions.

Exercise

Freewrite for 5 minutes on what you have learned about yourself and others in doing the icebreaking activities. Then share your piece with others.

Chapter Three

READING NOVELS
TO DEVELOP FLUENCY

If you want to become fluent in any language, you need a lot of exposure to it, and too often, this is impossible for ESL students. You can get great exposure to English through extensive, the kind of exposure most ESL students cannot get otherwise. Even you who are native speakers of English, to become fluent in reading, must read extensively. Too often, you have not read very much at all, and so you do not read fluently. But now you will.

1,000 Pages of Fiction

You and your classmates will read a few novels this semester, for a total of about 1,000 pages of reading. This may seem like a lot, especially if you haven't read much in the past. But it's only about **10 pages a day** for one semester. As you read so much, your reading will become more and more automatic, thus less and less difficult. Your vocabulary will increase, your spelling will improve, your understanding of grammar and idiomatic usage will advance, and all of this will occur without much effort because reading good novels is fun. Novels tell interesting stories and introduce us to fascinating people. They relate how these people live, love, think, feel, and often, die. They tell of their adventures, their mistakes, and their problems. They help us understand people and their problems.

The class will read the same novels so that you may discuss them and help each other to understand them. What's most important is that the novels will be entertaining and not too difficult to read, once you get into them. Reading them will also help you to write interesting stories.

You will do some reading in class, especially when you begin a new novel. The teacher will occasionally read aloud as you read silently. Usually you will just read silently. Each time you meet with your class, you will discuss what you liked, what you didn't like, what you didn't understand, and other things that interest or entertain you. To prepare for the first few of these group discussions, you should do the following:

1. Write at the top of each page of the novel a word, phrase, sentence or brief summary to help you remember what happened on that page.

2. Highlight or underline parts that you wish to quote or remember. Also highlight or underline vocabulary that you do not understand; then when you meet with your reading group, ask them (or your teacher) what the words mean.

3. For each class meeting, write 2 questions about the reading, 2 quotes from the book (parts that you thought were important or that you really liked or that confused you) on lined loose-leaf paper, and any new words that you think are important. Then share these in class.

Double-Entry Journals

After discussing the first few chapters with the types of notes I suggest above, you will begin keeping a double-entry journal. Each page will have a line drawn vertically down the middle, with parts copied directly from the novel on the left side, and your reactions on the right. Your reactions may include questions, challenges, opinions, analogies, inferences you make, musings, or conclusions you draw from the reading. As you write your journal entries, list words that are new for you, too. Then when you meet with your group, find out the meanings and use this vocabulary in your discussions of the book. That way your vocabulary will constantly increase.

Following is a sample double-entry journal page. Notice how the reader is talking responding to the things she is reading as she writes her responses.

Double-Entry Journal Sample
(from *The Great Gilly Hopkins* by Katharine Peterson)

COPIED	RESPONSES
"My name, Gilly said, is Galadriel."	*Gilly sounds very angry and mean. She also sounds like she thinks she's better than anyone else. She has probably hurt a lot of people. I wonder why. Maybe because she's angry about being in foster care. Or maybe she has been abused.*
"But I am not nice. I am brilliant. I am famous across the entire country. Nobody wants to tangle with the Great Gilly Hopkins. I am too clever and too hard to manage. Gruesome Gilly, they call me."	
"Well, 'scuse me honey," Mame Trotter said.	*I would not have been as polite as Mrs. Trotter if a new kid had corrected me so rudely.*
"You belong here now."	*Mrs. Trotter is really trying to make Gilly feel loved.*
"Well, we been needing somebody to rearrange the dust around here, ain't we?"	*Mrs. Trotter even forgave Gilly for being rude and dusting the bench before she sat down. She's really a loving person.*
Gilly gave William Ernest the most fearful face in all her repertory of scary looks.	*Gilly was so mean. What makes big kids bully little ones? I've never understood why this is so.*
She could stand anything, as long as she was in charge.	

Speaking of Vocabulary

You need not understand every word you read. If you understand the story line, but not some of the words, you can **infer the meanings** of those words **from the context** you read them in. And so, by just reading, you will learn new words without too much trouble because in novels, words are repeated often. If you also use the new vocabulary words in discussions, they will likely sink in. I also recommend keeping your own list of new words.

You and your classmates and teacher should collaboratively choose 25 new words each week from your readings, words that you all agree are important. You should study and be quizzed on them. Also, try to use these words in your written pieces: good vocabulary makes writing more specific and alive.

Activity 1: Write a double-entry journal page

Now take the book you are reading, read for a while and find some lines that you think are important, or that may be confusing to you. Copy those lines and then write your reactions on a lined sheet of paper divided in 2 columns.

Your reactions can begin with words like, "For me…" "I think…" "I like…" "I don't understand…" "I'm confused about…" "This reminds me of…" "Why did…?" "I predict that…" Afterwards, read your entries to your group, listen to theirs, and respond freely to each others' entries.

Activity 2: Share your journal entries in a small group

In class, **read aloud** a journal entry and your response to your group mates; let them respond as they wish. Then listen to their entries, and respond if you wish. This will get good conversations going about the novel.

Once you're well into reading the novel…

Activity 3: Play a Role

Take the part of one of the characters during group discussions, and speak as if you were that character about the plot, your motives, your feelings, your relationships with other characters, and more. It is a really enjoyable way to discuss and understand the books.

Activity 4: Write as if you were your character (point-of-view writing)

Write a piece as your character. Introduce yourself, but without revealing your name. Write a self-description, then explain your feelings and your version of what is going on in the book. Your teacher will hang up all these pieces around the room, and you will read all the pieces and try to figure out which character each piece is written by.

Activity 5: Write a letter to another character

Write a letter from your character to another, and try to straighten out a problem. Name the problem, analyze it and recommend a solution or explain why it can't be solved. Give the piece to that character, await his/her written reply, and write back until you two have straightened out the problem.

Activity 6:

Describe in writing how the other characters have misunderstood or maligned you. Write in self defense, and explain how/if you would change things if you could, and why you are right.

Activity 7:

Write to the readers, telling them how it felt as your character living in the time of the book, dealing with the other characters, and in the situation you were in.

N.B. This writing does not count toward your 10,000 word book(s).

Other Tips for Reading

Listen to the novel on tape as you read. It will help your comprehension.

Read the book with a classmate or two and take turns. Then discuss what is happening as you read.

Bring the novels to the beach, or park, or even on the subway or bus.

Read before sleeping.

But most important, read 10 pages a day, seven days a week.

Review Questions

1. How do we develop fluency in reading?

2. How did your discussions of the book go?

3. How do you like the idea of role playing as one of the characters?

4. Why do you think point-of-view writing is easier than other kinds of writing?

5. (How) do you think your vocabulary improved and will continue to improve as a result of reading discussions?

Chapter Four

FREE WRITING
TO DEVELOP FLUENCY

Free writing (Elbow, 1973) means what it sounds like: you write what you feel like writing and you do not worry about mistakes or pleasing anyone else. You will **free write every day for ten minutes** at the beginning of class. This will help you become comfortable with writing and write important, interesting things. It might also help you to produce some of the 10,000 words you'll need to write. Free write, too, whenever you feel like it.

However, **don't worry about making mistakes.** If you make a mistake, just cross it out and keep going. In 10 minutes, you will probably fill up an entire page, or maybe even two. Another reason for not stopping to correct is to prove to yourself that you can write a lot in a short period of time…you do have a lot to say! Free writing helps you to become comfortable with composing, which helps you to stop worrying about grades, neatness or correctness. When you are worried, your writing slows down and your ideas suffer. You cannot develop fluent writing if you are trying to write correctly at the same time. Fluency must come first, and lots of free writing about things you care about will lead to it. Correctness will soon follow.

Activity 1: Free write for 10 minutes, non-stop

Think of something you'd like to talk about on paper. If you can't think of anything, choose one of the topics below. Then write about it for ten minutes **without stopping.** It is important not to stop when you first begin free writing. It helps you to see that you can actually write a lot in a short amount of time. Look at the following free write for an example.

(Sample topics: How my parents met and fell in love; someone who's had a great influence on me; my favorite place; things I worry about; my future)

Free Write Example

My father was studying to become a priest, and so he had no plans to marry. Then, during his third year in the seminary, he got very sick with ulcers, and ended up in the hospital for several months. My mother was a dietician in that hospital, and so they became friends, but nothing more than that.

When my father was well, the seminary would not take him back; he was too much of a health risk. So he started a catering business and called my mother to ask her to work in his business. She agreed, and soon thereafter, they were dating and began to fall in love.

However, he told her he couldn't marry because he had to take care of his parents. She believed him, and started dating someone else. When my dad saw her with the new boyfriend, he proposed, and she accepted.

Activity 2: Reaction

When you have written for 10 minutes, stop. Rest your hand a minute or two, then skip a few lines and write for a couple of minutes how you felt when you were asked to free write and while trying to write without stopping. Share your reactions with your partner or class.

Activity 3: Share

Now turn to a partner and read aloud what you wrote during the free write. Sit next to your partner, so that s/he can read along silently with you. After you do this, your partner will read his/her piece aloud to you. Then tell each other what you liked or found interesting about each others' pieces. **Do not correct** or otherwise write on your partner's free write piece. Just respond. The teacher may ask a few students to share with the class how they felt as they did this first free write. S/he may also ask for a few volunteers to read their pieces aloud to the whole class. Don't feel embarrassed to share; it helps you to write better and to revise better. It helps you to realize, too, that writing is meant to be read by others.

Activity 4: Ideas for future free writes

Close your eyes and think of people, places, things and events in your past that you remember vividly. Write their names and a word or short phrase about them. Keep this list prominent in your writing folder; then you can refer to it for topics for future free writes. Next, think of your life now, and about the interesting, wonderful, scary, exciting or problematic things, events and people in your life. Think of places you love, people you love, fears, adventures, and other things that you know well. Add them to your list as you think of them.

Share your ideas with your partner or group and discuss them as you wish. Remember to keep this list in your folder to look at for daily free write topics.

Other Ideas for Freewrites

My opinion about (anything)

What I'm learning in _____

My worst nightmare

My mother (or) My father

What I learned from _____

A move I made

A love story

God

Life after death

Money and me

My worst fear

High school

When I feel/felt like an outsider

Where I grew up

My days as a child

Men

Women

A time I failed

My native country

Friends

What I'm really like

Going to college

Working

Getting married

Having children

Being single

Learning English

Learning to write

If I were rich…

Being thin/heavy/tall/short

Being young

Where I like most to be

A great moment in sports

Music in my life

A death that affected me

Advice to my children

Food and me

A hundred years from now

Dancing and me

The future

What I don't understand

An experience that changed my thinking

What I want out of life

Troubles I've had

The person I want to be

Places I dream of going or living

What my family values/believes

How the world should be run and how people should behave

What my mother/grandmother/father always used to say

Leaving country, home, family

If I were president of the US

N.B. Some of your freewrites can easily become part of your 10,000 word book(s), especially ones that are autobiographical or otherwise informative.

Chapter Five

WRITING NON-FICTION TO DEVELOP FLUENCY

Writing to Learn

A great way to learn new concepts is to write about them in your own words, as if you were explaining them to a friend. This is called "writing to learn" and it helps you to learn the concepts AND improve your writing. The reason is that you are writing in the way that you speak, so that new material becomes clearer and more memorable. So does your writing!

Activity 1

Start today writing what you are learning in other courses at the end of each class. You could begin with, "Today I learned…" and go on to explain as much as you remember and understand. When you finish, write questions about things you didn't understand. Ask those questions the next day in class. This is a powerful way to learn new material AND improve your writing. Following are some "writing-to-learn" examples.

(After biology class)

"Today in biology we learned that smoking, aside from hurting the lungs, also weakens the blood vessels and the heart, and can hurt the stomach, the mouth, tongue, throat, gums, nose and lips. It can cause cancer of any of those body

parts, high blood pressure and heart disease. What I don't get is how it hardens or weakens the blood vessels. It doesn't seem like the smoke or its products go into the bloodstream. How do they?"

(After Education class)

"The main reason why kids fail in school is that they can't compete with kids who already know more than they do. School is set up as a form of competition. So those who already know what they need to know in order to learn new material do so and get A's; those who have a little background to help them to learn the new material get B's; and those for whom the material is new get C's, D's or F's, depending on their background knowledge. Teachers grade students according to what they know, and they make assumptions about students' intelligence based on their grades. As a result, even by the end of first grade, most children can say whether they are smart, average or slow based on their first year in this competition called school. My question is, 'Why don't teachers know this and change it so that all children can succeed in school?'"

Now write for several minutes in your own words about what you learned in a class today, or what you learned in reading from a textbook, followed by any questions you may have. And don't worry about correctness or neatness. **DO THIS EVERY DAY** after every class; you will be amazed at how much you learn and how much your writing improves.

Interactive Writing

The following activities go a long way to develop fluency in writing, mainly because they are real and interesting activities, and not just practice.

Email Pals

Emailing with a friend or fellow student on a regular basis is a great way to improve your writing. As you attempt to write your thoughts clearly, your writing will become fluent and clearer. Your teacher may find another group of students

24

who are more advanced in writing than your group, and arrange for each of you to correspond regularly with a student in that class.

Dialogue Journals

Some teachers have their students write to them every day, and the teacher answers those letters. The student may be asked to write about the subject matter of the class, or just to write anything s/he wishes to. This is a great way to develop fluent and correct writing.

Keeping a Diary

Some people will love this; others may not. Writing a diary is a one-way, private conversation between you and your listener—the diary. It is a place to say things that you do not wish to say to people. In a way, it's like talking to a pet or a stuffed animal: it doesn't answer back. What is most beneficial is that if you write extensively in your diary, you will surely increase your fluency in writing. So I hope that you choose to write a diary and do it daily for at least 10 minutes. Who knows? It may become a big part of your 10,000-word requirement.

Silent Dialogue Writing

This is great fun, and a great way to increase your writing fluency. You and a partner decide on a topic that you're both interested in. Then you SILENTLY have a conversation on paper about that topic. You write your comment(s), then your partner reads what you have written and s/he responds in writing. Then you read and respond to what s/he has written, and so on. The only rule is that you cannot talk.

Activity 2

Spend a few minutes choosing a topic with a partner; then write a silent dialogue. When finished, talk about how it felt.

Telling True Stories

Here is a type of writing that can definitely be part of your 10,000 book(s).

Activity 3

Think of a true story that you heard in childhood. If you cannot, think of a more current true story. Write a list of the details in it; this will help you to write a rough draft. Or list the most important events in your story or vignette; then pick one, and write a list of things you see or remember during that event. It might be about a person you love or hate. Write a list of descriptive words, things they say, feelings they have, attitudes, habits, preoccupations, how they behave. Then write a vignette of the person in action in a specific scene, and work in some of the things on your list.

To start writing your story, choose one of the following: description of setting, character descriptions, character relationships, life stories, vignettes, dialogues (arguments, humorous exchanges, conversations, promises of love, etc.) or monologues (letters, speeches, recollections, diary entries, messages, soliloquys, dreams, memories), or even the conflict itself. Think about it for a while, using your **observational** and **creative** abilities. Then start writing that part and do not stop to make any corrections.

Take as much or as little time as you need, but **do not labor** over it. Pretend you're videotaping, and try to capture the essence of it.

When you finish, read it over and make any changes you wish, then read it to a partner for feedback. Revise as you see fit. However, do not write a rambling chronicle of not very unique life events. Here's an example. Read it and discuss how it is written and what you think of it. Then write your own story.

Lady (a true story)

My daughter's friend Priscilla lives in New York City, and for several years her dear dog Lady lived with her. Lady was a large, sweet canine, part German Shepherd and part Golden Retriever.

Lady was old for a dog, and one winter night, she died quietly in her sleep. Priscilla was deeply saddened, and she didn't know what to do with Lady's remains. She did not want to put her in the garbage, so she called her veterinarian and asked him what she should do. He told her to put the dog in a large suitcase and bring her to his office, just two subway stops away.

Priscilla did as he suggested, put Lady in her largest suitcase, and rolled it down to the subway entrance. When she got to the turnstile, she couldn't lift the suitcase; it was too heavy. A friendly fellow behind her said he'd help her, so she went through the turnstile and turned back to retrieve the suitcase. In a flash, the man darted away, pulling the suitcase behind him, another subway thief. Priscilla, speechless, began to cry.

She slowly turned and started walking toward home, and all at once her tears ceased with a big grin replacing them as she pictured the nasty thief opening the suitcase to find a big dead dog inside!

Other Stories You Can Write

Reporting the News: The Five W's

If you decide to write a magazine, a news report would fit in it very well.

You've probably read many newspaper articles on the latest war details, crimes, accidents, scandals, presidential decisions, space travel, fashion trends and Hollywood goings on. Recall how those reports try to give the most information with the fewest words. Newspaper reporters usually stick to the five W's—who, what, when, where, why—in reporting, so that readers get the most information in the least amount of time. For example:

Beloved Young Teacher Murdered for $40

Just before sundown yesterday, a young teacher returned home to the apartment he shared with fellow teacher, Vidal Perez, on West 130 Street in Manhattan. The door of the apartment was open, and just inside lay his roommate face down on the floor, his coat still on, and the back of his head shattered and bloody. In his right hand were his keys, and on the floor next to him, his school valise and a small bag of groceries. A bullet to the back of Vidal's head had killed him.

The police found an ATM receipt in Vidal's pocket; he had just withdrawn $40 from the bank. But the money was gone. They surmised that some low-life, likely a drug addict frantic for a fix, had seen Vidal withdraw the money, followed him home, and shot him as he entered his apartment, taking his money. The police believe that Mr. Perez was not aware that he was being watched or followed as he entered his building.

Mr. Perez, the only son of his parents ,Vidal and Maria Perez, and a native of Texas, was just 27 years old, and already a beloved teacher at Roosevelt High in the Bronx. Students and faculty there were stunned, as well as angry and grief-stricken on hearing of his brutal murder. So were his fellow students and faculty at CCNY, where he was pursuing a Master's Degree in Education...to become an even better teacher.

(This is actually a true story. It happened on Dec. 18, 2004.)

Sports Events

If you like sports, it is pretty easy to write about them. First read a few such pieces from newspapers and magazines to get an idea of how they're written. Then write a report of a real event that you have witnessed. To do this, watch the event and even videotape it if possible. Take notes on what happened, who did what and when. Keep score, and note the outcome. Then write your report and afterwards speculate in writing as to why things occurred the way they did. Illustrate your report with a scoreboard and/or pictures. And make sure you have covered the five W's: who, what, when, where and why. Here is an example, written by an eye witness, my husband, Ed Gilhooly.

World Series Perfect Game

At the age of 15, I saw baseball history in the making. It was October of 1956. Don Larsen of the New York Yankees pitched the first and only perfect game in World Series history. Before a sold-out crowd at Yankee Stadium, Larsen faced 27 batters, with no batter reaching base by way of hit, error or walk. The last batter he faced, Dale Mitchell, a life-time .312 hitter, struck out. With that, pandemonium broke out, and Yankee Hall-of-Famer catcher Yogi Berra leapt into the arms of Don Larsen.

The game was in doubt from beginning to end. The pitcher for the Brooklyn Dodgers was the legendary Sal "the barber" Magli, so called because he used to pitch perilously close inside. He surrendered only two runs, and pitched a beautiful game.

Don Larsen was lucky that he won the game. Five Hall-of-Fame players were in the Dodgers' line-up: Roy Campanella, Jackie Robinson, Peewee Reese, Gil Hodges and Duke Snyder. At one point, Gil Hodges, Hall-of-Fame first baseman for Brooklyn, hit a tremendous drive to left center field. Yankees Hall-of-Famer Mickey Mantle—the fastest center fielder of his time—raced to his right, and barely caught the fly ball in the webbing of his glove in deep left-center field.

In another unusual play, Brooklyn's Hall-of-Famer and fleet-footed Jackie Robinson hit a sharp ground ball between 3rd base and short stop. It looked like it would clearly go through for a hit. The Yankees' third baseman, Andy Carey, dove to his left, and while parallel to the ground, got the tip of his glove on the ball. The ball ricocheted to deep shortstop, where it was fielded by Gil MacDougal, who made an off-balance throw from deep shortstop to throw out Robinson going to first base. Had either of those balls gotten through, it is quite likely that the Yankees could have lost. What a game! Even as I write about it for you, I re-live the thrill it was to be there that day.

"How-To" Writing

This entails writing clear steps explaining how to do or make something. It is a series of steps of some process. For example:

How to Get an "A"

Getting an A in a course is not that hard, even if the subject matter is. First, pay close attention in class and take good notes. If you can't keep up with the notes, bring a small tape recorder, sit close to the instructor, record the class, then replay it at home to complete your notes. Second, right after class, write what you learned and any questions you have. Then ask them in class the next day. Third, don't just read the textbook; study it. As you read, make an outline of the most important material, or highlight it in the book. Then study those parts. Fourth, get all your assignments in on time, and make sure you do a complete job. Fifth, study with a classmate or a group of classmates on a regular basis. Talking about the material with others will help you to understand and remember it better. And sixth, when studying for a test, create likely test questions and answer them fully. Then rehearse those answers. Doing all these things will practically guarantee an "A" for you.

Feature Stories

Feature stories focus on a person, place, event or issue of public interest. Full of facts, they often include interview material and pictures. They give readers an insider's view, rather than just the straight reporting of the five W's. Feature stories about people include information on why the person is famous (or infamous), personal data, and the person's work. Feature stories on issues may include a few pieces, like a report, an interview, illustrations and an editorial piece. Look at feature sections in popular magazines like *Time* or *U.S. News & World Report,* and the following.

The Butchers of Iraq

Stories of the sadistic cruelty of Saddam Hussein, former president of Iraq, are so horrific that many people simply refuse to believe them. Nonetheless, they are true. Aside from ordering mass murders of hundreds of thousands of his own countrymen, he delighted in watching his enemies being tortured and dying slow, agonizing deaths. Many times, before he tortured and killed his enemies, he would have their wives and children raped and then tortured to death, making his enemies watch and hear their screams, helpless to do anything. He would have their nails pulled out, burn them, electrocute them, have their eyes gouged out and have them viciously beaten. He also ordered people to be boiled in oil, put through human-sized shredders, dismembered, set on fire alive, and other nightmarish acts. And he would laugh as they screamed in pain. He often brought his two sons to the prisons to enjoy watching people being tortured and killed; they would watch and laugh as they ate their lunches.

Saddam Hussein and his sons are/were sociopaths. Sociopaths feel no guilt or sympathy for the suffering of others. Saddam Hussein grew up with an abusive stepfather, who beat him often and delighted in making his life miserable. Maybe that somewhat explains his behavior, but what about his sons? What's their excuse? Their father loved them; they were never abused. Yet they became rapists, tyrants, and murderers.

They went on to torture and murder thousands more innocent people, with neither pity nor remorse. They were sadists like their father, as they seemed to enjoy others' screams from pain. They were incapable of feeling guilt for their deeds, much less sympathy for those they brutalized and murdered, their widows and orphaned children. Their evildoing knew no bounds.

Advice Columns

In these columns, the advisor/writer prints a letter from someone needing advice, usually on etiquette or affairs of the heart. Then s/he writes advice to that person. Check the Dear Abby column to see examples like this:

Dear Abigail,

I need your advice. My husband has a terrible temper, and lately it has gotten worse. When he is angry, he throws things and yells, which scares the children, who are only two and four years old, and they start to cry. Before they were born, he used to just shake me or push me when he was mad. But now he has started to slap me in the face and on my shoulders and back. And last night, he made a fist and punched me in the stomach. I was unable to breathe for a few moments, and my stomach still hurts. He apologized, and has apologized before. So he knows it is wrong. I think if he gets a better job, he will be less frustrated. But in the meantime, I am worried that he will get more violent. What should I do?

Hurting in Boston

(reply)

Dear Hurting in Boston,

You are standing in the path of an oncoming train. You should either have your husband removed from your home with a restraining order from your local law enforcement agency, or take the children and go somewhere safe, like your parents' home. Escalating spousal violence often ends in terrible injury or even the death of the victim. Throwing things and yelling is one thing; deliberately hurting someone who can't defend themselves is much worse. Do not delay; leave before anything worse happens. Then seek the help of a family counselor. Go! Now!

Abigail

Chapter Six

DEVELOPING THE
CRAFT OF WRITING

As you write real stories and creative ones toward your 10,000-word goal, to make them interesting and even memorable, you must work at the craft of writing. A craft is something you work on with your hands, your mind, your imagination and your emotions. In writing, you do this by revising.

What is writing? How do we develop as writers?

First, let's talk about what writing is and what it is not. Writing is not a matter of pleasing teachers, avoiding errors, or being neat. Nor is it something that only a few people can do well. Writing is a language and thinking process which ends with a written product, and you can be successful at it.

Just as you learned to speak through lots of interaction with others and by concentrating mainly on **meaning** and not worrying about making mistakes, you can also develop writing. The difference between writing and speaking is that what you put down on paper is the **only** thing that your readers have; that is, they must grasp your intended meaning or follow your ideas from only what you have written. You will likely not be next to them to clarify things if they do not understand. So it must be as clear as possible.

Writing is also far more succinct than talking. And there are no gestures, facial expressions or intonation to help a reader understand a written text. Whereas in speaking, there may be false starts, interjections, corrections, and repetitions, writing does not have these supports. Thus, the writer's full meaning must be in the text s/he writes.

A popular misconception about writing is that very few people can learn to write well. However, **anyone can learn to write well by working hard** at it, **getting others' help** and **persevering.** First, you must trust yourself that you have interesting things to say. You must also write with the same conviction and energy that you use when you talk. Your readers should not only read what you think, but hear you as you write—the unique way you have of expressing yourself—so that your writing sounds like you. That said, let's look now on how we will work during our daily writing workshop.

Rules for Writers' Workshop
(adapted from Nancie Atwell, *In the Middle,* Boynton-Cook, 1988)

1. When you are writing, there should be no erasing; just draw one line through anything you might ordinarily erase. You may want to use what you cross out later.

2. Write on one side of the paper only and on every other line. Then you may add material and/or cut up your piece to reorganize it.

3. Save everything you write, because to become an effective writer, it's necessary to understand your own processes of writing and not to throw out "gems" by mistake.

Date and label everything you write. e.g. family dinner piece, draft #2, March 5. Or "notes" 4/3, "research summaries" 11/2.

Speak quietly when you work with partners. It is important for you and your classmates to be able to think as you plan, write, revise and edit. You can't do that if others' noise is distracting you.

Work really hard. Be creative. Pretend that writing is your livelihood. That will make you work hard on your piece.

Speaking of Partners...

When we write, we try to get our intended meaning down on paper, hoping that it is interesting and easy to read. But sometimes, we don't succeed. A great way to see if your writing is interesting and easy to follow is to read it to someone else and get that person's feedback. So let's give it a try.

Activity 1

Spend twenty minutes writing two paragraphs, and use the following openings: in paragraph #1, "I used to be..." and in paragraph #2, "But now..." Once you have finished, read it silently to yourself and make any revisions you wish.

When everyone is finished, the class will sit in a full circle. Everyone will read their pieces to the whole class, and the rest will listen. After each piece has been read, those listening will write down one **observation** about the piece—not a criticism, nor a compliment, nor a suggestion.

You will each **write just an observation:** something you noticed, something that stood out in the piece, like "I noticed that the middle was really interesting" or "The first part was surprising." After a piece has been read, one by one everyone will read their observations aloud to the author. The author should listen and take notes for possible revisions later on.

Activity 2

Write now what you think are some helpful observations you can make after you listen to a fellow student read a piece. Then brainstorm your responses with the class and add some more to your list. Remember, you are like fellow authors helping each other to be creative and interesting. Compare the list your class generates with mine (below); there will likely be some overlap. Discuss why all these responses might be helpful to a classmate. Discuss, too, responses that would not really be helpful to a writer.

Other Helpful Responses

I really liked…

I'd love to hear more about…

I'd love to know why…

I noticed that…

The way you…was really memorable

I'm a little confused where you write…

Could you describe…a little more? I can't really picture…

That's a great word you used here. It shows, rather than tells, your meaning.

This sounds like…

Tell me more about…It's so fascinating.

Is there something missing…? I'm a little confused.

You should definitely publish this once you clear up the rough spots.

You're repeating yourself here.

Could you think of a more descriptive word than "good?"

Activity 3

Read to a partner any piece you've written for your 10,000 word project. Then ask your partner to use any of the above expressions to respond to what you've written. Take notes so that you'll remember his/her comments. Later on, they will help you to revise (improve) your piece.

Then do the same for your partner. Have him/her read a piece to you, and then you should respond to the piece using some of the above expressions. This will help your partner to revise his/her piece.

Noticing Authors' Techniques

We learn a lot about writing by reading. As you read your novels, you will become familiar with how people write effectively. Try to notice at least one of those techniques every day that you read, and note it in your journal to mention to your group members. Look for:

How the author begins paragraphs

Character descriptions

How the author describes places, things, smells, sounds, and surfaces

How the author describes action

How the author includes dialogues and monologues

How the author writes chapter beginnings and endings . . . .

How the author leaves some episodes unfinished

Notice how the author reveals what the characters are like, especially contrasts and conflicts, inner motives and feelings. Here are some contrasts that an author might develop:

honest vs. dishonest	brave vs. cowardly	good vs. evil
straightforward vs. elusive	weak vs. strong	kind vs. mean-spirited
educated vs. uneducated	trusting vs. suspicious	innocent vs. corrupt
antagonistic vs. conciliatory	verbose vs. laconic	positive vs. negative
scheming vs. guileless	truthful vs. mendacious	serene vs. tormented

People often reveal their characters as they speak. Things like cynicism, honesty, cowardice or bravery can surface through one's talk to oneself and others.

Activity 3

Go through the pages of the book you are currently working on—only the pages you have read so far—and find some examples of **monologue.** Read these to your reading group and discuss the "voice" of the person whose monologue it is: i.e. discuss how his/her personality, attitudes, hidden and overt agendas, etc. come through in the monologue.

Activity 4

Next, try to find some **dialogue** revealing the voices and characters of two or more people. Discuss how the author weaves together action and character development.

Activity 5

Now look for some straight **description.** It might be of the character's physical appearance, character, mental state, motives, or emotional state. Discuss how the author wrote this description with your peers.

Activity 6

In these monologues, dialogues and descriptions, how does the author develop contrasts between and among characters? Discuss these contrasts with your peers.

Activity 7

As you read your books, notice how authors begin scenes, how they end them, where they leave you guessing, and generally how they manipulate you into wanting to keep reading the book. These are techniques that make a piece of writing interesting.

Look at the pages you have recently read in your novel, and find some examples of how the author begins paragraphs, scenes or chapters. Does s/he leave unanswered questions, go back to the past, or go forward? List some of those beginnings, then read and discuss them with your reading group. Then look at how the author ends scenes and chapters. Does s/he leave readers guessing and wanting to find out what happens next? Try to figure out **why** the author is structuring the plot in this way.

Activity 8 (from Atwell, *In the Middle*)

Read the first paragraph below, then look away and try to picture what you have read. Then read the second, third and fourth paragraphs, and see how much more memorable they are. Discuss each with your classmates.

Typical

It was a day at the end of June. My mom, dad, brother, and I were at our camp on Rangeley Lake. We had arrived the night before at 10:00, so it was dark when we got there and unpacked. We went straight to bed. The next morning, when I was eating breakfast, my dad started yelling for me from down at the dock at the top of his lungs. He said there was a car in the lake.

Action: A Main Character Doing Something

I gulped my milk, pushed away from the table, and bolted out of the kitchen, slamming the screen door behind me. I ran down to the dock as fast as my legs could carry me. My feet pounded on the old wood, hurrying me toward the sound of my dad's voice. "Scott!" he bellowed again.

"Coming, Dad!" I gasped. I couldn't see him yet—just the sails of the boats that had already put out into the lake for the day.

Dialogue: A Character or Characters Speaking

"Scott! Get down here on the double." Dad bellowed. His voice sounded far away.

"Dad?" I hollered. "Where are you?" I squinted through the screen door but couldn't see him.

"I'm down at the dock. MOVE IT. You're not going to believe this," he replied.

Reaction: A Character Thinking

I couldn't imagine why my father was hollering for me at 7:00 in the morning. I thought fast about what I might have done to get him riled. Had he found out about the way I talked to my mother the night before, when we got to camp and she asked me to help unpack the car? Did he FIND THE FISHING REEL I BROKE LAST WEEK? BEFORE I COULD CONSIDER A THIRD possibility, his voice shattered my thoughts. "Scott! Move it! You're not going to believe this!"

Writing Effective Lead-Ins

A good lead-in can "hook" your reader into wanting to continue reading. The lead-in can make the reader curious, entertain, or touch him/her emotionally. It can also help you, the writer, to write the rest of the piece.

Activity 9

Discuss the three effective lead-ins on this and the previous page, especially what makes you want to read on.

Details, Details, Details

You need to show your readers what you see as you are writing a piece, by giving them the details that will allow them to see it. You need not give every detail of every scene or person, but enough for your readers to see and feel and hear, and even to smell what you want them to.

Activity 10 (from Calkins, *The Art of Teaching Writing*)

Read the following smaller paragraph, and discuss with others what you see or feel as a result. Then do the same with the longer one.

Draft 1

I was at a beach in Florida. I pressed my toes into the hot sand. I saw my sister jumping out in the waves with my aunt. She was jumping around as the waves hit her. She was out deep...I wanted to go and play in the big waves with her, but I was nervous to.

Draft 2

I pressed my toes in the hot sand. I wiggled them around. The gritty sand felt good on my sunburnt toes. I looked out over the ocean. My sister was out deep, jumping over the waves with my aunt. Sometimes the waves got too big and they would knock her over. Then my aunt would put her up, and she'd be dripping wet, and they'd start laughing. My shoulders were hot from the burning sun. I would have loved to be out there in the waves, but I was too scared.

Keeping a Writer's Notebook

Have you ever had a great idea or question that you didn't want to forget, and then you forgot it? It happens to most people. However, if you keep a little notebook in your pocket and **write in it any time you have an idea you don't want to forget,** you will have a little gold mine to draw from as you do your writing for your 10,000 word project. So start your writer's notebook and keep it with you.

Other Tips for Writing Well

1. When you write, don't be afraid to use your imagination.

2. Be active in class, especially in your discussion groups.

3. Ask for help whenever you need it, and help others when they ask.

4. If you have access to a computer, use it to write your pieces.

5. Think of your class as a literacy club which you have joined to have a good time and to improve yourself. Be as active in that club as you would in any other. Then you'll be really pleased.

Chapter Seven

WRITING OUR LIVES
TO DEVELOP FLUENCY

Writing Your Life Stories

Why write life stories? First, because we know so much about our lives, and second, because it is great to have those stories to read in the years to come. It's also easy! You will be surprised at how much there is to tell about your life. I suggest writing a series of vignettes—or short stories—which capture the most important events, places, people, and issues in your life. Or you could combine the story of your life with a political history of your country.

Getting Started

Getting started is easy: just write the names, places, and people most prominent in your life, and then write associations you make in thinking about them. For example:

HOME: Santo Domingo, warm, bare feet, music, the smell of dinner, blue Caribbean waters, sandy beaches, brothers and sisters, my bed…

MOTHER: beautiful smile, cleaning, talking with father, caring for baby, listening to me after school, cooking, laughing…

THE EARLY YEARS: feeling secure, playing with siblings, best friends, projects, escapades, favorite things, accidents, fears, heroes, heroines, hideouts, dreams, nightmares, learning to get along with others...

THE TOWN: police, old folks, neighbors, church, school, stores, roads, events, trees and flowers, typical days...

BIRTHDAYS/CELEBRATIONS: parties, games, presents, cakes, music, dancing, decorations, anticipation...

SCHOOL: favorite people, easy/difficult work, fears, traumas, happy times, ballgames...

ME AT AGE _____: shy, anxious to make friends, skinny...

OR: Start with Lists

1. MAKE A LIST of the events, decisions, and relationships that have shaped your life, things like births, illnesses, deaths, moves, fires, tornados, floods, famines, accidents, the community you grew up in, the religion you were raised in, your important relationships (romantic, or with relatives, friends, teachers, employers), a failure or success, love relationships, marriage, children, career choices, spiritual experiences.

2. Now WRITE SOME POSSIBLE HEADINGS, and group all the items from your list that can be grouped under an appropriate heading; for example:

Early years	Moving	School	Tragedies	Marriage
Mom	leaving home	failure	grandma	being in love
my room	goodbyes	English	missing	new home
playing	flying	the fight	jobless	babies
siblings	strangers	best friends	9/11	money
church	culture shock	learning	car crash	traditions

3. NARROW YOUR LIST to those relationships, decisions or events that have been **crucial,** those that made you a different person and made the most difference in your life. These will probably be the richest source of material for writing your memoirs. You can write about them as whole stories, or write vignettes, scenes, dialogues, or descriptions, all full of details you remember because these have been so significant to you and others.

Life Story Questions

Following are some questions from the Southern Oral History Project that may help you to decide on what to write about. **You do not need to write about all of them**...just the ones for which you have the best material. I suggest you do some free writing on the ones that really call up strong memories. That writing will likely turn into one of the pieces you will work on to include in your "book."

Life Story Questions

Childhood

1. What are your earliest memories? What are your fondest early memories?

2. What do you remember about grandparents or other relatives?

3. Whom did you spend the most time with? What did you do?

4. Did anyone you were close to die? How did you react?

5. What was your home like?

6. How did your parents deal with you and your siblings?

7. What kinds of games did you play; what toys did you play with?

8. Who were your neighbors? Did you have friends?

9. What were your other childhood activities?

10. What were family meals like?

11. What were other family routines?

12. Describe religious training in your home.

13. Describe a momentous event in your childhood.

14. What fears did you have as a child?

15. What were your family's most important ceremonies?

16. Who did the most/least talking at home?

17. Did your family ever move?

18. What were the family rules for conduct; what was the family philosophy?

19. Were there new babies in your household?

20. Were there elderly relatives? How were they cared for?

21. What happened when you or others became ill?

22. When your parents were out or away, who took care of you?

23. If a parent or a close relative was out of work, who helped him or her? Was there outside help from charity or the government?

24. What was your room like? Did you have a favorite place?

25. What person do you remember most vividly from childhood?

26. What was school like for you as a child?

Here is a piece about #25.

Grampa

Grampa looked like a grampa. Balding on top, he wore round spectacles, suit trousers, and a vest with a pocket watch and chain. He had little bumps and wrinkles on his face, along with a perpetual smile. Grampa also acted like a grampa. He would smile and sometimes laugh with joy when I ran into his arms. He would hold my face in his hands and tell me how pretty I was. Sitting in his favorite chair, he would put aside his newspaper and read to me anything I wanted for however many times I wanted.

When I visited my grandparents in their 3rd floor walkup, I'd watch at the window and wait for him to come home from work. As he plodded up the street, empty lunchbox in hand, I would call to him and he'd wave and smile at me. I'd watch him eat his dinner, always with rye bread and butter, as he listened to all my news and complaints of the day.

He never took me anywhere, and I don't remember him giving me any presents. I just remember feeling really special, and really loved, whenever I saw him.

Your parents

1. What work did your father and mother do? What did they say about it?

2. Did your parents read and write much? When, what, where?

3. What kinds of things did you talk about at the dinner table?

4. Did your parents spend a lot of time with each other? Did they talk with each other a lot? About what kinds of things?

5. What were your parents' priorities?

6. Did your father and mother have friends? Describe them.

7. Which parent were you closer to? Explain.

8. Who made the major decisions in the family?

9. Who took care of the children? And their discipline?

10. What did you like to do with your parents?

11. How old were your parents when they married? What was their education?

12. What conflicts did your parents have?

13. What activities did they participate in outside of the home?

14. What was their attitude about your friends, dating, courting, moving out, marrying?

15. How were money issues handled by your parents?

16. What kind of entertainment did your parents go in for?

17. Did you ever see your parents grieving? How did you feel?

18. What do you think your parents did wrong in child rearing?

Here's a piece about #7

She Was There

Though I loved my father, I was always closer to my mother. She was always there, and she was predictable. She got us up in the morning, made our breakfasts, packed our lunches, then bundled us up, rushing us off to school with a kiss. She was there when we got home, with snacks and a standing order to go out and play, and not to come in until our cheeks were rosy. By sundown, dinner was ready, usually meat, potatoes, vegetables, bread and milk, often with canned fruit for dessert. After dinner, the girls helped to clean up, and the boys put the garbage out. Next, we all sat at the kitchen table to do our homework. She would help those who needed it and check to see that everyone's homework was complete. If we finished early, we could go to our rooms and read or play, but no TV was allowed on school nights. Lights were out by 9:30, but first, everyone said their night prayers, the youngest with her help.

Mom was there for every sports game we played, every play or concert we were in. She loved music and had a beautiful soprano voice. She sang along with Broadway show music, popular love songs, and even operas. She taught us to tap dance, do the Charleston, and even waltz. Everyone's birthday was cele-brated with a cake and presents. And when we came home from a day in school, she would delight in listening to our stories and complaints. She loved to laugh with us, and consoled us in sadness. She went to church and prayed for us every day. Whenever we needed it, she was there with good advice. When we grew up and left, it pained her, but she was still always there when we needed her. And when our children needed her, she was there, too. We all miss her a lot now that she can no longer be there.

Adolescence

1. Were sports important to you?

2. What about music?

3. When did you begin to consider yourself grown up?

4. What were your closest friends like?

5. What did you do together?

6. Discuss what school was like: the work, the people, etc.

7. What was your opinion of yourself as a high?schooler?

8. What were your main extra?curricular activities?

9. If you got in trouble at home or school, what happened?

10. Did your parents want you to pursue a certain occupation?

11. What did you want to be when you grew up?

12. Were you ever treated unjustly, unkindly in school? At home?

13. What were your feelings about the opposite sex then?

14. When did people stop treating you like a child?

15. Were you expected to behave in certain ways around adults? How about when you were around members of the opposite sex?

16. Did you have a job? What did you do with your earnings?

17. How were you disciplined?

18. When did your siblings or you leave home? Was it traumatic?

Here is an example of an adolescent reminiscence, #16.

Sitter for Six

The summer before I turned 13, I had grown to my full adult height of 5'9" tall. And so my mother thought I was ready for a job. I had heard of a young mother of six needing help, and so I applied. I told her I was experienced in child care, which I was, and 14 years old, which I wasn't. And so I got the job: 9 to 5, five days a week, for 50 cents an hour.

The children were aged 1, 2, 3, 4, 5 and 6 that summer. When their parents went out, I would be in charge of all six of them. But on most days that summer, their mother and I would take the children to the pool. She would take three and I was to make sure the other three didn't drown. It was very hard to keep three little heads above water. After a frantic few hours helping them to survive in the pool, I was relieved to go back to their home, bathe and dress them, and put them in for a nap.

On some days, I would baby sit in the evening as well, when the parents went out for a break. That included cooking dinner for the six, feeding them, and clean-up. Next, of course, they wanted to play...with me! Sometimes they would get silly and play tricks on me, and then there were always the fights over toys and other disagreements that I had to referee. Happy hour for me was bedtime at 8 o'clock. I don't think I've ever had a harder—or happier—job.

Your social self

1. How do you define your social class? Explain.

2. How many years of schooling have you and our family member had? What kind of jobs do you and they have/aspire to?

3. Do you have more schooling than your parents? Your friends?

4. To what ethnic group do you belong? What cultural, and/or linguistic group?

    How does this identification influence your thinking?

5. What do you know about your family's roots?

6. How do you think other groups in society view your group?

7. What are the stereotypes your group holds of other groups?

8. What kind of problems were/are there in the society in which you grew up? What was/is their effect on you?

9. What kind of education did you have? Did you do well in school? What do you remember about your teachers and learning?

10. Is education important in your social group? What is important?

11. What social and geographical mobility do you have?

12. Could you improve or change your social class? Will you?

13. What language(s) do you speak? Read? Write?

14. If you speak more than one language, when/where/with whom do you speak/read/write each language? Explain as fully as possible.

15. What kind of literature did/do you like to read? Why?

16. Are you comfortable interacting with people from other ethnic, cultural and linguistic groups?

17. What historical forces and/or events affected your family's present status and history?

18. What are your parents' values and beliefs? Do you still hold them?

19. What expectations did/does your family have for you?

20. Have these expectations changed due to outside forces or events?

Here's a sample piece based on #18

My parents' values were hard work, honesty, responsibility to help the poor, and loyalty to God and family. Father and mother of eight, they believed in God and went to daily mass to worship and to pray for their children. At home, we all said prayers of thanksgiving before and after meals, and we prayed the family rosary. On Sundays, the whole family went to church together. On week nights, we did homework and read, and on weekends we could watch TV, play, and socialize with friends.

My parents expected us to study hard, be respectful of other adults, and help with the housework. When we were old enough, we were expected to get jobs and save our money to help defray college expenses.

We were punished if we lied, cheated, answered back or were otherwise disrespectful. One command we feared was, "Go to your room," especially on weekends. If our grades fell below a "B" average, we were not allowed to go out with friends until the next marking period. Our parents emphasized the impor-

tance of obtaining a good education. They encouraged us to do our best in everything, but mostly, they stressed being kind, generous to the poor, and committed to our religion.

Adult life

1. What transitions have you made in your life?

2. When did/will you marry? Where? With what kind of party?

3. How did you meet your spouse? Describe your spouse.

4. Did you need your parents' approval to marry?

5. Did you move out of your parents' house while single? If so, where/how did you live?

6. Did/will you have children? When? How many?

7. Who takes/took care of your children?

8. Did/do you raise your children the way you were raised?

9. What is your household like? Do you own or rent?

10. Did/do you/your spouse work? Where? When? Doing what?

11. How do/did jobs affect family life?

12. If separated or divorced, when and why did it happen?

13. What are your adult routines, rituals, and customs?

14. What is your opinion of people you work with?

15. What are your plans for the future?

16. Do you have a plan for retirement?

17. Do you and your spouse communicate about feelings and hopes?

18. What do you talk about regularly?

19. What kind of time do you spend with your children?

20. What are your hopes, fears, etc. concerning them?

21. What are your religious beliefs and practices?

22. What are the similarities and differences between your parents' values and attitudes, and yours today?

23. What conflicts are you experiencing as an adult?

24. What disillusionments have you experienced?

#22

Recently, my sister sent me a small dish with the inscription:

Mirror, mirror, on the wall.
I am my mother, after all.

I laughed about how, after all the complaints I had had about my own upbringing, as an adult, I find myself having the same values, beliefs and behaviors of my parents, even though at the time, I thought they were wrong about almost everything.

I have heard myself say things, like "You either get B's or you're grounded until the next report card." How I hated those words when I was in high school! I also ask my children, "Am I as fat as that lady?" just like my mother used to ask me. I say they should listen to my advice because I'm "older and wiser" than they are. And I talk about how much their father and I have sacrificed for them...just like my mother did. Yes, I am my mother, after all. She'd be so happy to know that!

Your psychological self

1. What kind of a person are you?

2. What things do you value most?

3. What kind of disposition do you have?

4. What are your basic beliefs?

5. Try to characterize your behaviors.

6. Do you understand yourself?

7. Are you happy, troubled? Why?

8. What is your philosophy of life?

9. How do you see other people? How do you think they see you?

10. If you could change one thing about yourself, what would it be?

Other Pieces to Write about Your Life

Family Stories

These will come easily. These are stories you have told before, probably more than once. They might have happened on family vacations, or when you were little, or at the dinner table, or on the beach, or during a family party or disagreement. Take a mental photo of the event and describe the details: Who was there? Where were they? What were they doing/wearing/saying? What were the sounds, smells, tastes, textures, feelings of the scene?

Letters to Family

Write a letter to someone, alive or dead, as if you were composing a real letter. Ask questions; share your thoughts and feelings. Then answer your letter as if you were the person you had written to, sharing your thoughts and feelings. Your subconscious will help you out.

Disturbing Memories

Write in a private place—a journal, for example—and explore some problem or disturbing memory, issue, loss, or person. Write about difficult things that have caused you pain, but only for as long as you feel comfortable doing so.

People you Know/Knew Well

Do this patiently and in great detail. Use specific, unique details about their looks, their facial expressions, posture, walk, gestures, clothing, activities, talk, feelings, what was important to them, what they thought of others, how they treated others, their daily activities and concerns, their personalities, their flaws, and how they did things, and reacted to events and people, how they lived and how they died. Tell little stories about them so that people can experience them as you did.

Conclusion

You could spend a lot of time writing your life stories. And it would be time well spent. It will be up to you and your teacher how much of your 10,000 word project will be autobiographical. Let me state again that it's good to write a variety of pieces: factual, autobiographical, reflective, creative and so on. These could comprise your "book," and be called "The Collected Works of (you)" or you could write your life story/stories, a novelette, and a magazine.

Chapter Eight

DESCRIBING PEOPLE, PLACES & ACTIONS

Describing People

Part of telling a good story is giving your readers the ability to **see** your characters as you do. To describe a person, you need good details. You can choose among age, size, shape, color (hair, skin, clothing), textures, voice, walk, posture, odor, facial expressions, gestures, and unique physical characteristics (moles, scars, tumors, eye patches, nervous twitches, obesity, frailty), and other details like neatness, cleanliness, peculiarity or distinguishing details of dress. Don't tell all of them, but just the ones that really stand out and "show" the person. Try to appeal to your readers' senses, too: sight, smell, touch, hearing, and even taste.

Activity 1

Think of a person you can **see** vividly in your mind. Close your eyes if you have to and really look at that person. Pick out the things about him or her that stand out the most in your mind. Then write a **physical** description of that person, including bodily details, and details about clothing, posture, and other physical characteristics. When you have finished, close your eyes again and **see** that person. Look for important distinguishing details that you have missed...ones that you would definitely include if you were drawing a picture of that person. Now add these to your written description.

Try to describe the person's way of speaking and otherwise interacting with people. This will lead to further description of the person's emotional or psychological state, education, and even their character. Some adjectives you might find useful are: withdrawn, pensive, shy, soft-spoken, guarded, inebriated, fearful, suspicious, loud, joyful, dramatic, bubbly, confident, self-conscious, shaken, steady, forceful, weak, sly, straightforward, cocky, guileless, self-effacing, down-to-earth, unassuming, elusive, talkative, curt, abrupt, friendly, spontaneous, direct, demure, outspoken.

In short, try to describe what that person is like: mood, character, speech, disposition, behaviors, values and other characteristics. Give enough details to help the reader to get a good idea of the kind of person you are describing. You might want to make a list of adjectives first; then continue writing your character description.

Activity 2

To practice description, write a few pieces or paragraphs on three or four of the following topics. Describe (i.e. give a physical description of):

    a person with a bad cold or flu
    a police officer or a military person
    yourself
    a famous political or military leader
    a person you love
    your ideal marriage partner
    a favorite teacher
    a crime suspect as the police might describe him or her.
    a character from your neighborhood
    a serial murderer
    a crazy person
    an alcoholic, a drug addict, or a derelict
    an exaggeration of a person
    a sickly, dying or dead person
    a person who is angry, depressed, or otherwise upset

a scary person

a person in a play, movie, opera, or T.V. program

a person you admire from a distance and would like to know

a child

a character in the novel you plan to write

Read each piece you have written to your writing group, and get feedback on it. Then revise it to make it as interesting and vivid as possible.

Describing Places

Just as in describing a person, to describe a place well you must be a **good observer.** You must not only see all the details of a place, but be able to pick out the ones that will most vividly **let your readers see it** as you do. Your readers should not only **see** the place vividly, but should feel it as you do or as you wish them to. Thus, you may add **actions** to your description of a place: who's doing what, what's happening, where people are located, what people are saying, and so on. Appeal to the reader's senses: sights, smells, textures, noises, and ambience. Try to capture these with descriptive words, and with language that specifies size, shapes, location, activity level, and the combination of all of these as setting.

Activity 3

To practice describing places, start with where you are right now: your classroom. With a partner, write as complete a description of it as possible...enough so that an artist might be able to sketch it from your description. Then try to write a description of the atmosphere or ambience of the place. Remember, you want your readers to feel like they are there. Before and while you and your partner are writing, discuss details and actions. Then try to write them as precisely and evocatively as possible, capturing the ambience of the place as well as a pretty exact description of it.

Activity 4

Now describe a place you have very strong feelings about: you might hate it, love it, fear it, be disgusted by it, or have fond memories of it. Describe it physically, with action details that would give a sense of its emotional meaning to your readers as well. It could be your home, a subway, a park, a cemetery, a room, a church, an office, a business place, a factory, a battlefield, a government office, a restaurant, an athletic facility, a street, city or town, a beach, and so on. Read this piece to your partner for feedback. Revise it until you think it paints the place well and evokes in your readers the feelings it evokes in you.

Where Am I?

Another way to build your descriptive vocabulary is to play the game, "I'm thinking of a place" and have people listen to your description and guess where it is. The place should not be an easy one to guess, but should allow the listeners to have fun and enjoy the competition as they strive to be the one who guesses the place. Let me give you an example or two.

#1

I'm thinking of a place that is stark white. It is round and there is nothing else to see except the white contours surrounding me. It is all the same, whether I look up, down, to the right or to the left. And it is a place where I can only stay for a few minutes, lest I die of suffocation. I can tell if the sun is shining or if there is artificial light outside of this place. The whiteness of it becomes even brighter. But if it is dark out, this place is penetrated by darkness, and the whiteness of it is barely discernible in the darkness. It's a bit difficult to stand in this place because it is completely round. And one more thin: to fit into it, I must temporarily shrink to the size of a bumble bee or a lady bug. A butterfly or a mouse would be too big. If I try to run inside of this place, it will move round and round and round. Where am I?

#2

I'm thinking of a place where there is never any sunlight. Many people come and go from there every day. Sometimes the crowds are so big that you can barely move, but must go with the flow of other bodies. There are pungent smells of filth there: dirt, rotten garbage, smoke from cigarettes, cigars, marijuana and engine exhausts, odors from loiterers who haven't bathed in a long time, and the grit and grime of years of neglect. The place is relatively barren, with a few benches, pillars, and walls that have absorbed too many coats of dingy paint. There are discarded newspapers and other refuse scattered here and there, and there is graffiti everywhere. Some of it is obscene; the rest is political, personal or simply absurd. Art it is not. The place is usually pretty quiet, filled with strangers who do not talk to or even look at each other. Then in the distance one can hear the thundering approach of wheels and a monotonous pre-recorded announcement. Where am I?

(Answers: #1, Inside a ping-pong ball; #2, NYC subway station.)

Activity 5

Write at least one descriptive piece of a place or scene, choosing from the following topics. Then share the piece(s) with your group and revise it/them.

the report of the scene of a crime or accident.
a teenager's bedroom.
an imaginary planet.
planet earth from the viewpoint of an extraterrestrial being.
the inside of a computer, radio, T.V., car engine, etc.
a mother's womb from the viewpoint of her unborn child.
a prison cell.
a supermarket, a toy store, or a fresh air market.
a morgue or a funeral home.
a hospital operating room.
a neighborhood or a section of a city.
a museum or a church.

a zoo or a farm.

a dream house or a favorite hiding place.

an abandoned building or a garbage dump.

ancient ruins or modern cities.

the world from the top of a skyscraper or a jet plane.

what you see as you travel through a place

your first impression of the United States or of New York City.

a tour through a place.

the evening sky or the earth at dawn.

Describing Actions

When you describe places, it's good to also describe actions (what is going on) and feelings. When you described your classroom, you probably included actions like, "students quietly writing," "the teacher surveying her pupils as they work," "most students engaged with their own creativity," or "everyone wondering if they're doing as well as their peers." Describing your campus, you might include actions like, "students leisurely strolling and chatting excitedly with friends," "bright banners flapping from upper floor windows," "fallen leaves being shuffled here and there by the wind," "a game of touch football blocking traffic," "a few student activists passing out pamphlets," and other descriptions of actions. You might tell feelings, like "happily dodging a stray ball." Let your verbs do the describing.

Activity 6

To start describing actions, first try to describe the actions involved in some simple routines. Write out an exact description of someone doing two of the following actions:

getting into a car, starting it up, and driving away

smoking a cigarette   washing dinner dishes

preparing a meal   eating a meal

Activity 7

Next, give precise written directions for someone on how to do something you know how to do. Here are some suggestions:

    how to bake a cake or some other recipe
    how to fly a plane or drive in a busy city
    how to type without looking at the keyboard
    how to play soccer, basketball, football or another sport
    how to meet and marry the person of your dreams
    how to rob a bank, hijack a plane, or escape from prison

Read your pieces from Activities 6 and 7 to your group and get their reactions. You might find that you have left out some important steps. Revise your pieces to make them complete.

Activity 8

Now pretend you are a newspaper writer and report on one of the following. Describe it and then speculate on its impact, importance, the human element, or other aspects of interest.

    an athletic event
    a social event
    a crime
    a war event, an accident or a disaster
    a political or governmental event

Read your piece to your group and revise it, but do it as if you were preparing to publish it in a real newspaper or a magazine. Illustrate it if possible. When finished, talk with your teacher about publishing it in class or elsewhere.

Activity 9

Write about the event that had the greatest impact on your life, whether happy, sad, traumatic, or ordinary. When finished, read to your group and revise as usual.

Why Is Action So Important?

The heart of a story is the action: from actions that are described as characters move, talk to one another, gesture and make facial expressions, to major episodes in the plot. To describe actions, we not only answer the five "W" questions— who, what, when, where, why—but we add enough **descriptive detail** for the reader to see the action as we see it.

The key to writing effectively about action is **observation.** You must be a keen observer of things you really see or things you imagine if you are writing creatively. Make real pictures in your mind of the characters, scenes and actions, and then describe the actions as they happen. Try to see them in **slow motion** if necessary, in order to capture the details that will make the reader see the actions as you see them. And remember to add other details of **description, talk or mental state** that complete the description of the action.

Activity 10

Think of some action you have observed and are familiar with. For example, a bank robbery, a surgical operation, or an accident you witnessed, a skating performance, a person getting ready for a big date, someone making something, a child at play, a baby feeding herself, a sporting event, a fight, a brush with danger, a terrorist takeover of an airplane, a scene at a beach or park, a scene of a person receiving bad or good news, a car chase, a dinner table scene, a shy person trying to make a friend, a crazy person talking to her/himself, a funny mishap, or a mysterious-looking person and what you observed him/her do. Now write about one of the actions with as much description and action as needed. Remember to use action verbs, ones that really show the action.

Chapter Nine

POINT-OF-VIEW WRITING
TO DEVELOP FLUENCY

One of the most enjoyable ways to freewrite is to **write as if you were someone (or something) else:** a character in a book, a political figure, a religious leader, a movie star, a sports hero, a war hero, an historical figure (king, queen, slave, caveman, cavewoman, explorer, etc.), an animal, an object (e.g. a computer or a building), your mother, your father, a friend, a relative, a crazy person, a doctor, a person from another country or culture, a building, a tarantula, an angel, or a super hero.

From this new "point of view," you could write a letter, a speech, a diary entry, a challenge, a report of what happened, an essay, a poem, a song, a threat, a monologue saying what's on your mind, a prayer, a critique, a sermon, or whatever you wish. You have artistic freedom since you are someone else writing.

You could write a letter from someone in the past to those living now, or to another person from the past. You could write to your future children, or to ancient ancestors. You could write your secrets, or unfold a mystery. You could write messages from a military leader of the past. Or you could explain how it was to live in a certain era in the past.

For example, you could write a letter from Christopher Columbus to present-day Americans, or from your great-great grandparents to yourself. You could write a news report in the year 2100, or how it feels to be a one-year old not yet able to talk. Or write to someone in the past and point out how he or she should have done things differently.

Point-of-view writing is really fun and allows you to be very creative. It has been my students' best writing, and I think the reason is that they can use their imagination to the fullest, and not worry about reporting accurate facts. And fantasy can be much more powerful than reality. That power can come out in point-of-view writing. And of course, since it is freewriting, you need not worry about neatness or errors. Look at the following example, then try some point-of-view writing as anyone—or anything—you like. Have fun!

My name is Christopher Columbus. In 1492, with the help of their majesties Ferdinand and Isabel of Spain, I set out to sea with my crew and hopes to discover a Western route to India. You see, at the time, I thought the world was round and a bit smaller than it is, and that if I traveled west, I might get to India faster than traveling east. Well, I was certainly mistaken.

After a few hard months at sea, we arrived at an island we thought was part of India, and so we called it one of the West Indies. We called the natives there Indians, although they didn't much look like the Indians of India. Anyway, our mission was successful, so we thought, and it didn't take long to get there!

Later we found out that this island was not a western part of India, but that there was a whole continent, another huge ocean and lots more land before one could reach India. Even so, I was proud of our discovery.

We called the island Hispanola, and when we returned to Spain, we brought new spices, fruits, plants, and even some natives to show the king and queen. Little did I know then that we had discovered a whole new world. Now I am dead, but so proud that a country, Colombia, has been named after me, and that the day of our discovery, October 12, is now a national holiday in the United States of America.

More Ideas for Point-of-View Writing

A letter from your stomach (or your heart) to you
A diary entry your first girlfriend/boyfriend may have made

A speech your mother would make if she were president
A sermon you would make if you were a preacher/priest/rabbi
What a baby would say if he/she could talk to you
What your pet thinks of you
A chapter for a history book about happenings during your life
Your report as a psychiatrist of someone's behavior/problems
A telephone conversation two world leaders might have
What you feel like as a blind person
Letters from leaders of warring countries to each other
An interior monologue of a person on his/her first date
A description of you as someone else sees you
A letter Jesus, Mohammed or Moses would write to us today

Point-of-View Writing Activities

Following are some sample point-of-view openers. Use your imagination and finish the paragraphs. Try to be the character from whose point of view you are writing.

When finished, share your work with classmates to see who has been the most inventive. I think you'll find out that point-of-view freewriting can be very entertaining.

1. Most people don't understand what it's like to be a dog. But as a dog, I...

2. You might remember me. My name is Abraham Lincoln. I'd like to tell you why...

3. Movie stars like me are so misunderstood. People think...

4. Living on Mars is far different from what earthlings believe. We Martians...

Chapter Review Questions

1. How do we develop fluent writing?

2. What happens to our writing when we try to avoid making errors?

3. What is more important, composing or being correct? Why?

4. What is freewriting? How does it promote fluent writing?

5. What is point-of-view writing? How does it promote fluent writing? What else does it allow a writer to do?

Chapter Ten

WRITING YOUR "NOVELETTE" OR SHORT STORIES

We all enjoy reading or hearing a good story. Stories may be about conflicts, joys, fights, romances, embarrassing moments, mysteries, funny incidents, tragedies, racist episodes, children's pranks or activities, and just about anything else. They are slices of life that can be read in a relatively short time. Characters in short stories and novels can be everyday ordinary people or mysterious or powerful people. This chapter will help you to write your novelette or some short stories.

What Makes a Good Story?

Whether you are writing a memoir or a creative story, good stories have some things in common. They have a plot with a beginning, a middle and an end. A conflict is stated, a main *character* or *characters* are introduced, there is *rising tension or action,* perhaps complicating the conflict, a *crisis, falling action* and a *conclusion.* The conflict is a problem; what your characters do or say or what happens to them is the action; the crisis or climax is where things fall apart or come together. The conclusion resolves the problem.

A good story helps your readers to see your characters, hear them, see the action, and find out or infer the conclusion. The drama of your story entertains your readers, drama emanating from the characters, the action, the setting, the dialogue, the suspense, the familiarity, or the strangeness. A good story also focuses on only one set of characters, actions and settings.

A good story has specific, striking details, not abstract words and phrases. The words mean exactly what you want your readers to see, hear, smell, taste. And no words are wasted. It also has a point of view, or the perspective of the narrator, which helps achieve certain effects and set the tone of your story. It is written like a vignette, which may or may not make a larger plot, as if in separate "takes" when someone is producing a movie. The climax comes fairly soon; and the action is quick, not dragged out.

Finally, a good story is all there; there are no gaps. When you read it to others, you do not need to explain it. If you do, something is missing and you need to go back and revise it. And it is written in fairly predictable ways.

Story Skeletons

Stories, long or short, have familiar skeletons, or shapes—ones which readers expect and enjoy. I'm sure you'll recognize some of the following skeletons.

Boy meets girl. They fall in love. A big problem threatens to keep them apart. They fight it. It looks like they are going to lose each other, but in the end, they get together.

Country A attacks Country B because it wants to build an empire. It enslaves the inhabitants of country B. Country B patriots form an underground resistance movement. Through many exploits of bravery, they finally manage to liberate their people.

An ordinary vacation turns into a nightmare when terrorists (or extraterrestrial beings) take over the resort hotel in which the protagonist is staying. S/he must find ways to overcome the terrifying situation.

Twelve people are invited to be dinner guests at a huge unlived-in mansion on a rainy night. The electricity fails and the lights go out. When candles are found and lit, the group discovers that one of them has been murdered. The group is stranded at the mansion because all the roads to it are impassable. They must spend the night there. During the night, there is more murder and mayhem. You must find the murderer.

Creative Writing? Me??

Yes, you! You can write creatively, believe it or not. You could write a fictional autobiography (pretending you are someone else), a romance, a mystery, an adventure, a science-fiction story, or an historical story. Or you could combine details about your real life with a fictitious story. As you try your hand at writing fiction, you will likely find yourself relying on many experiences you have really had and associations you have made in life.

Activity 1: Try your hand at telling a scary story

Write a scary story, and let your imagination run wild. Think of something that will horrify your readers. You could write a true story or invent one, as long as it is horrific.

You could write about the scariest dream or experience you ever had. It could have been something you imagined as a child lying in bed in a dark room, or a real event which threatened your life. It could be about real world events or other-worldly. It could include bats, werewolves, ghosts, zombies, thieves or murderers in the night, stranglers lurking in hallways, falls into deep abysses or from high cliffs, monsters, poisonous or mind-altering potions, vampires, a kidnapping, being chased by a murderous maniac or being lost in a scary place with strange sounds. It could take place in graveyards, underground tunnels, foreign countries, abandoned dungeons, dark basements or attics. Or you could write about a dream that was so bad that it woke you up. But try to capture those things that horrified you.

When finished, read the piece aloud to your group. Answer any of their questions, get their advice, and then revise the piece as needed (move material, add some, delete some, expand, etc.). As you read the piece aloud to your partners, you will find things that you want to change. Do so, and then continue reading. One reason for reading to your partner is for you to clear up confusions, add missing material, or delete unnecessary material. Reading aloud and having an audience helps you revise things yourself.

Write Stories in Parts

Most writers have a general skeleton in mind, but begin their story by writing parts of it, rather than having the entire plot worked out. By writing these fragments, they are building a story, but often still may not know what the whole plot will eventually look like. Fragments could be descriptions of people, places and actions you see in your mind, conversations you imagine, letters you feel compelled to write, etc.

You might do well to write your stories in this way—in fragments—rather than try to follow a plot you have already decided on. It is more fun, and it feels like less work, if you write vignettes or fragments, rather than sticking to a predetermined plot. In the end when you put your story together, you may decide not to use one or more of these fragments, or maybe you will use them all. (I'm sure, by the way, that your teacher will include them all in your 10,000 word requirement!). And by the way, you may start out wanting to write a novel, but then as you write, you may decide on a collection of short stories instead. Allowing yourself this freedom will enhance your creativity as you write.

Activity 2: Begin with settings and characters

If you can't think of good story fragments to write, why not begin with the setting and characters? Try to imagine the setting vividly in your mind: to see it, to hear the sounds there, to smell it and to feel it. Within this setting, you could begin introducing your characters. Write first their physical descriptions and then start to describe the relationships among the characters.

Activity 3: Tell the conflict

Now move quickly into the conflict, whether it's territory, money, love, jealousy, good vs. evil, invasions, crimes, injustices, or something else. Describe actions surrounding the conflict, and write dialogues with arguments, promises of love, humorous exchanges; and monologues: messages, letters, memories, soliloquys, descriptions of dreams, and even speeches. Sometimes it is even necessary to write brief life stories of characters in order for your readers to understand what made them what they are today, or brought them into the circumstances of the story.

Structuring your Story

The joy of suspense

A cardinal rule for writing is: **Do not bore your readers.** You can shock them, scare them, make them laugh, make them cry, make them remember or see something beautiful, make them think, make them feel guilty, righteous, uncomfortable or secure, or make them hate or love something. But don't make them yawn or not want to continue reading.

You can sustain your readers' interest by the content AND the way you structure your story or book. One of the great joys of reading, watching a movie, or just hearing a story told is the **suspense,** the wondering about what will happen next. It is no accident, therefore, that a writer plans to give the audience the excitement of suspense…of suspending them for a while in uncertainty and guessing while other parts of the story, character descriptions, monologues, or dialogues occur. I'm sure you've experienced suspense in your life: a kind of delightful uncertainty where you must try to figure out what will happen next.

To build this suspense into your story, you must structure it in such a way that your reader's knowledge builds gradually, but there are still many unanswered questions. A fictional plot usually begins with a complication of some kind; then comes a crisis, and then an untangling of that crisis (the denouement).

Activity 4

Think of the book you are currently reading: how has the author built up suspense? What do you know? What things are still unknown to you that you are anxious to find out? How has the author accomplished this? What did s/he tell you first, second, etc.? Discuss these questions with fellow students, and why you still want to read on.

Now let's look at how to write mystery stories.

Writing a Mystery Story or Novelette

(adapted from *Teaching and Writing Popular Fiction*)

Some of the most enjoyable reading is mystery reading. As we read mysteries, we try to discover secrets: who committed the crime, how it was committed, the motive, the concealment, and the unraveling. Mysteries are full of unexpected surprises and turns. The writer keeps us guessing until the very last. Mysteries keep us on the edge of our seats because generally they include fear, secrecy, violence, a victim, clues, darkness, chases, shootouts, captures, trials, convictions and other things that ordinary people are scared of. The criminals involved are unique. They do terrible things that we would never dream of doing.

Those who solve the crime are also unusual people. They take great risks, have unusual insight, have to survive by their wits, and have to figure out the truth from bits and pieces of seemingly unrelated evidence. They also have to notice things that escape the ordinary person. They have to be above suspicion, yet know about the evil workings of the human mind. They do not have to look heroic (tall, dark, handsome men; or beautiful women), but they do have to act heroically when necessary, and outwit their suspects.

How Mysteries are Written

Generally speaking, first there is a crime: a murder, a robbery, a kidnapping, arson, or another serious crime. There are also various people: victims, detectives, policemen, eyewitnesses, character witnesses, suspects, and possibly gangsters or hit men. There are things like guns, fingerprints or pieces of hair or skin, knives, footprints, scribbled messages of victims, things left behind by the criminal, and other clues to the crime. Then there is the pursuit: surveillance, chases, shootouts, fights. This is followed by the capture or surrender: handcuffing, reading of legal rights, booking, arraignment, and incarceration. Then come the trial, witnesses, testimony, prosecution and defense, the verdict and sentencing.

Once the crime is committed, someone often tries to conceal it. The detective looks for clues and follows suspects to see if they give him any leads in solving the crime. He suddenly finds he is in danger. He either escapes or fights it out with the suspect and wins. This way he solves the mystery. Often there is a confession or a tacit understanding of the guilt of the suspect through his/her actions at the end.

Some mysteries begin when a corpse is found. Others begin when an innocent person is accused of a crime, or witnesses a crime. As the sleuth tries to solve the crime, with or without the help of a sidekick, s/he sees things that ordinary mortals miss. S/he knows that even when a case is air-tight, there is something amiss. Following intuition and hunches, s/he solves the mystery.

Witnesses or victims struggle through anonymous threats on their lives (mysterious phone calls, letters, shots through their windows). They come home to a wrecked apartment. They pour over mug shots in police records; they sit behind a one-way mirror and view lineups of suspects. Some shady witnesses attempt to blackmail the criminal instead of reporting him or her. Meanwhile the detective is interrogating everyone, studying clues, and taking notes (mental and/or physical) on the various pieces of the puzzle.

Often, a romance is woven into the story. The detective and an innocent witness being sought by the criminal fall in love. He protects her, but she must be brave and in so doing, helps to solve the crime. The detective is constantly vigilant and constantly asking questions...of himself and others. In the end, he solves the mystery, there is a trial, the criminal is convicted and sentenced, and if there is a romance, they get married.

Writing an Adventure Story or Novelette

If you like adventure movies—about wars, death-defying feats, ocean voyages, treks across wildernesses, espionage, science-fiction, people facing terrible odds, interplanetary or intergalactic conflicts and the like—you will probably enjoy reading and writing such stories. Look back over your writing so far. Which piece(s) did you feel most comfortable with?

Your adventure story or book could be about a hunt for buried treasure, man against nature, a kidnapping, a race, a rescue, an escape, a battle, a competition, a chase, or an intrigue. Your protagonist could be trapped somewhere, taken prisoner, mistaken for the wrong person, abandoned in the wilderness, caught in a storm, being pursued by killers, captured by aliens or desperately trying to survive somewhere. Maybe s/he is trying to save the country from disaster, to find a kidnapped president, to help people survive a plane crash in the snowy mountains, or to prevent some terrible disaster.

There might be car chases, fights, torture, lack of food, sleep or water, darkness, fear, and loneliness. Your hero or heroine might wake up a different person, or only two inches tall. S/he might be trying to uncover the mysteries of the Bermuda triangle or the sinking of a great ocean liner. Perhaps in a foreign prison or an alien land, your hero/heroine might be trying to escape or outwit his or her captors.

An adventure story is one of a test of the protagonist's strength and wits against formidable odds and opponents, whether nature, people or superhuman beings. Your protagonist is probably looking for a person, a place or a thing. S/he has to kill or capture or rescue a person or people. As the protagonist pursues this goal, enemies put terrible obstacles in his way. The hero/heroine must overcome these obstacles. S/he must also be brave, strong, clever, resourceful and idealistic.

Your protagonist will be on a journey or a crusade to make right a wrong. He or she may explore, discover, or transform things. Your hero is also likeable and trustworthy, and never gives up. The action will leave your readers in suspense: there will be tests for your protagonist, and terrible odds to overcome. But in the end, despite setbacks, s/he will overcome any obstacle. (Partially adapted from *Teaching and Writing Popular Fiction,* by Hubert.)

Writing Science Fiction

If you enjoy science fiction stories or adventure/science fiction, you might enjoy writing one. Watch some science fiction movies—new ones or ones you've seen before—but this time focus on **how** science fiction stories are developed.

In science fiction, the theme is usually deals with human reactions to radical changes in life as we know it on earth. These changes will probably include technological ones, and may well include sociological, psychological and philosophical ones as well. There also may be time warps, space warps, threats of destruction, robots, androids, alien forms of life, and lost worlds. There is usually advanced technologies, exploration and often colonization. And often there are new sociological and cultural situations as a result. The characters often encounter new faiths and religions, and sometimes changes in the psyche.

The setting may be on earth or another planet, or in space between celestial bodies. The scenery, however, will be very different from our own surroundings, and the human characters will react to them.

Science fiction characters usually take intergalactic or interplanetary trips in spaceships that are propelled at great speeds. They are comfortable traveling throughout the cosmos. There is usually a male protagonist who is heroic and a born explorer and warrior. The female protagonist is beautiful and feminine, and very resourceful. Like the male protagonist, she is strong and adventurous. The other characters serve to enhance the importance of the protagonists, and have much lesser roles and importance. But the opponents are very important, creating the tension and suspense in the story. They are the complete opposites of the protagonists.

The beginning chapters will tell the five W's: who, what, when, where and why. They will tell when, where and why the story is taking place. They will introduce the major characters, and describe the relationships among them. Then there will be a circumstance or event, a crisis, that will give rise to conflicts, complications, minor clashes and steadily rising action. There may be threats, challenges, then battles, intrigue, narrow escapes, and the use of every form of technology possible. The action will intensify and it will be hard to tell who will win.

Then there will be a major climax with a crucial encounter. Here problems are finally resolved; mysteries are explained. Throughout the protagonists will have some victories but just as many setbacks, because struggle is the essence of science fiction. But in the end, s/he or they will prevail, and will have a new world or a new vision or dream.

Writing a Love Story

A romance is the story of a relationship and the feelings associated with it. It tells about how people meet, get to know one another, get close, separate, reunite, start again and deal with conflicts until love prevails and they remain together. Romances usually contain tests of the couple's love for one another: tests caused by jealousy, forced separations, and other obstacles. A romance may be combined with a mystery or an adventure story. It may even be combined with a comedy, but the is focus will be mainly on the relationship.

There may be a romantic setting, or one that is mundane. But there is often a loneliness in the protagonists, a sense of expectation, and a longing for love. The protagonists are good people who deserve to be loved. They may also be good-looking, but this is not required. The hero may be the strong, silent type, and the heroine demure and sincere. Or they may both be comedic. But both are trust-worthy and likeable.

The story usually begins with their meeting, then their physical descriptions, then their getting to know each other through actions or through accounts of their pasts, then physical overtures toward each other, closeness and declarations of love. After this, their love is usually tested with obstacles, like temptations, rivals, jealousy, rumors, or conflicts over money, relatives, betrayal, or each other's pasts. There may be quarrels too. The suspense builds as the reader wonders if the romance will last. There may be fears, anger, sadness and yearn-ing. But in the end, love prevails, there is exaltation and fulfillment. The hero usually proposes marriage to the heroine, and they live happily ever after.

Some romances build up within an adventure the couple is involved in: solving a murder mystery, espionage, a journey, a catastrophe, or a war, for example. Readers enjoy the combination of emotion and excitement in such stories. But even in these stories, the romance is just as important as the other part of the plot.

People in love have poignant dialogues, write to each other, write in their diaries, fantasize, and see beauty in each other. They are strongly attracted to each other, and often suffer when they are apart. The trick is to describe these feelings with dialog and descriptive passages, while keeping the action moving. In addition to choosing romance as your genre, you have to think of the type of romance you will write about. Romance stories can be very uplifting, the kind of fairy tale stories that are a pleasure to see, read, and write. See some of those movies before you dismiss romance as a genre you might be comfortable writing in.

Writing a "Point-of-View" Autobiography

It is great fun to write a "point-of-view autobiography," an autobiography as if you were someone else: a deceased person, a living person about whom you know a lot, or an imaginary person. This is, in my view, the most enjoyable and creative experience in biography writing. It allows you complete artistic freedom, challenges your imagination, and is usually the most entertaining form of biography to read.

Chapter Eleven

DIALOGUES, MONOLOGUES, & OTHER COMPOSING TECHNIQUES

Writing Dialogues

Through conversations or dialogues with people, we come to know how they think, what they've done, their plans, their disappointments, their hopes, and their fears. People's words also reveal their priorities and their preoccupations. They can help to tell what's happening in a piece of fiction, relationships among characters, and conflicts. And for writers, dialogue writing is one of the most enjoyable, creative forms of writing.

Activity 1

To begin experimenting with dialogue writing, write down a real dialogue that you have heard between two other people. It doesn't have to be written word for word; it should just sound like a real conversation. Write the dialogue as you see it written in novels. But first, read and discuss the differences between the two dialogues below:

> *"Where did you get that gun?"*
> *"None of your business."*
> *"I demand to know. Where did you find that gun?"*
> *"I didn't find it. I borrowed it."*
> *"Whoever lent it to you is the murderer."*
> *"What? But that's impossible!"*

"Where did you get that gun?", she demanded angrily.

He coolly replied "None of your business," putting the gun into his pocket.

"I demand to know," she said, shaking him bodily. Her lips tightened and her eyes narrowed with anger, "Where did you get that gun?" She knew it was the murderer's.

"But that's impossible," he retorted, the color draining out of his face.

Now read your dialogue to your partner and ask him or her if it sounds like a real dialogue. Or you might want to write a dialogue **with** your partner, with each of you taking a role. Then discuss whether it sounds like a real dialogue.

Once you've finished, go back and add any descriptions of **how** the lines should sound, and other necessary material, if just the dialogue alone doesn't do the trick.

Activity 2

See if you and your partner can develop a dialogue into a one-act play with a complete plot. Try to write it with as little **talk** between yourselves as possible. That way, what you write will contain the meaning you both intended. Then when you're finished writing, discuss where you need to revise the lines of the play and revise it. Then get a few of your peers, as many as there are parts, and read/act out the play. Let them tell you also where there might be improvements.

Activity 3

Now with your partner, write two pieces. First, write a dialogue that reveals the characters' inner selves and motives.

Next, write a dialogue revealing a conflict. It could be between two leaders of warring nations, or two neighbors with a conflict. Make it realistic.

Talk about the characters and the action before you write. But once you start writing, keep the talk between you and your partner to a minimum. Try to write at least one of the pieces on your own. After both, read, discuss, and revise them with your partner.

Writing Monologues

A monologue, or one character talking (alone or to others), is another wonderful way to develop characters and plot. Some monologues are stream-of-consciousness types, whereas others are like little speeches directed to the reader or a group. They are also a way to reveal the thoughts of a character. And most important, they **sound** like the character: they are written in the character's way of talking and thinking. They are also typical of the character's personality.

Actually, you have already done a great deal of monologue writing by freewriting in your writing journals and writing your double-entry journal entries. Monologue writing is also a way of thinking on paper. Your monologue writing reveals your feelings too: anger, impatience, self-confidence or lack thereof, frustration, exhilaration, confusion, etc. Well, in fiction writing, you may use monologue writing in many ways: a confession, a speech made by a character defending him/herself, a diary entry, a person talking to herself or himself, a self-analysis, a request for help or understanding, talking through a problem to try to resolve it, a self-portrait, feelings of not belonging or of inadequacy, a first-hand account of an event, a dream, or even a whole or most of a novel or play told in first person. To write convincing monologues for characters, you must really feel sympathetic toward them, and get inside their heads. It's hard to write convincingly if you do not do this.

Activity 4

Try doing some freewriting to get some ideas for monologue writing. Focus on your own thoughts first. First freewrite, describing what is going on in your own mind right now: thoughts, scenes, apprehensions, plans, and so on. Then think about how one of your characters in your book, or yourself in your autobiography, can reveal so much about him or herself through this type of stream-of-consciousness writing.

Activity 5

A good technique is to talk to yourself. Do a freewrite talking to yourself on paper: giving yourself advice, reminding yourself to do something, getting angry at yourself, patting yourself on the back, complaining, or whatever you ordinarily do when you talk to yourself. (Even if you don't talk to yourself out loud, most of us talk to ourselves in our minds.) Just write the talk that's going through your mind.

Another type of monologue is to have a conversation **with yourself**…an actual dialog you have with yourself, with two sides of your personality talking to each other: the wise side to the foolish side, the saver to the spender, the romantic to the practical, and so on.

Read your monologues to your partner, get feedback, and revise them as needed. Discuss with your group the advantages of writing dialogues and monologues into your stories.

Chapter Twelve

REVISING

By now, you have done so much reading and writing that you have achieved considerable fluency in writing. You have gotten your ideas down on paper in interesting, comprehensible, complete and logical ways. This is a great accomplishment. Next, you can work on improving your writing by revising it.

What is Revision?

Revising has been called "the real work of writing." It means **looking over what you have written and improving it as much as you can.** When you revise, you can add, delete, move, correct, or otherwise change material to make your piece more readable, more complete, clearer, more interesting, or more memorable. You can change words to better show your readers what you mean. Important advice about writing is, "Show; don't tell." This is what you will try to do as you revise.

Revising is not to be confused with editing. Editing is correcting mistakes in your writing: mistakes in verbs, spelling, punctuation, quotations, prepositions, negatives, articles, run-on sentences, sentence fragments, and so on. A good way to differentiate between revising and editing is to think that revising is what real authors (people who write for a living) do; editing is what their secretaries do.

Why Revise?

Almost no one writes a perfect piece the first time around. That's why you have been asked to read aloud your project pieces to others and get their feedback in order to consider making some changes. Revising with others' help eventually helps you to revise well on your own.

Revising for Completeness, Comprehensibility & Flow of Ideas

A priority in revising is making sure everything you need or wish to say in a piece is there, and that you haven't left out anything important. The flip side of this is to delete any unnecessary sentences, phrases or words. Since we're first concerned with fluency, remember these criteria: **A fluent piece is comprehensible, complete, logical, devoid of gaps or unnecessary material, and engaging to read. It should also have a discernible beginning, middle, and ending.** So go over your piece for these qualities before you read it to a peer for feedback.

Responding to Writing

We have already discussed effective ways to respond to another person's piece of writing (see p. 30). However, the first, most basic issues you should respond to are:

comprehensibility (i.e. Is the piece understandable, from beginning to end?)

completeness (Is everything in it that needs to be in it? Or are there gaps?).

logical flow of ideas (Does anything seem out of place?")

Respond to these three things first, with comments like:

"I don't understand........."

"What do you mean when you say......?"

"Is something missing here?"

"Did you mean to put this here?"

Activity 1

Take a piece that you have written on every other line and one side of the paper only, read it aloud to a classmate, get feedback, then revise it. Make sure it is 100% understandable, that you have included all important information, and that you delete any unnecessary material. See if you have a discernible beginning and ending. And make sure your ideas flow logically. That is, revise the piece for fluency.

Responding to Another's Writing

The point of collaborating with peers is not to criticize each other, but to help each other to compose better. Furthermore, **responding does not mean correcting.** Your responses should focus on composing.

The author should read the piece aloud, and the respondent should listen and read it silently at the same time. The respondent should stop the reader when confused, or if the author has read something that isn't on the paper or skipped something that is.

Let's go over the kinds of responses that can help someone to revise (improve) a piece of writing. First rule: All responses should be constructive, not destructive. Second rule: comprehensibility, completeness, and logical flow have to be addressed.

If the piece isn't fluent, that must be addressed first.

If a piece is already fluent, you should begin your responses by indicating the strong parts of a piece: what you liked best, what you found memorable, what you learned, or good feelings you had while reading or listening to the piece. Your reactions can begin with words like, "I noticed...," "I really liked...,"

"This reminds me of," "What I find most memorable is...," or "What sounds best in the piece is..."

After you tell your partner honestly what you liked, what you learned, and why you wanted to read on, address the rough spots with words like, "I don't quite understand...," "I would really like to hear more about...," "My question(s) is/are...,"

"Your focus seems to be...," "or "If this were my piece, I would..."

On the next page is a revised piece. Notice that the author doesn't erase the original text, but simply puts a line through it. This is done in case the author decides later on that the original wording was the best choice. Also notice how the author writes on every other line, making it easier to revise. The writer will usually revise as s/he reads the piece to a respondent, as well as after the reading.

Even Weaklings Can Stop Smoking

One reason you should stop smoking is that it might kill you. Smoking is not a healthy practice. It might kill your family members, too. It is a waste of money. Cigarettes are very expensive these days. But smokers have a terrible time giving up smoking. They say that it is ten times harder than going on a diet. And anyone who has gone on a diet knows that dieting is extremely hard. And like dieting, once you give up smoking, it is hard to maintain that abstinence. I heard once that ninety-five percent of dieters regain all the weight they lose. And I read somewhere that in the case of alcoholics, only five percent of those who join Alcoholics Anonymous stay with the program; the others resume drinking. Then I have also heard that alcoholics say that giving up smoking is harder than giving up drinking. Well, all I know is that I smoked between one and two packs a day for many years. Then I got pneumonia and had to stop smoking or lose a lung. After about two weeks, I never wanted a cigarette again. And I am a certified weakling: I can't diet, I don't exercise, and I am basically a couch potato. If I can give up smoking, anyone can. All it takes is a good old healthy fear of dying.

Revising Paragraphs

Breaking your pieces into paragraphs makes them much more readable because paragraphs give the reader's eyes a break. They also chunk material into reasonable thought groups, helping the reader to comprehend the piece. What's most important about paragraphs is that they seem to be right in the **context** in which they appear. That is to say, they should go well with the paragraphs preceding and following them.

A paragraph is supposed to group together related sentences. When people read these units, or groups of sentences, it helps them to remember what they read.

Paragraphs also say and do something. So a good way to check your paragraphs is to answer these questions for each one: "What does the paragraph say?" and "What does the paragraph do?" You should be able to briefly summarize what it says. If you cannot, perhaps it says too much and should be divided into two or more paragraphs. Then answer what it does. Things that a paragraph can do are to explain, illustrate, restate, introduce, give proof, restate important things, conclude, and so on. Once you do this for each paragraph, you'll have an outline of your piece. Go over this outline to make sure that the piece flows as you want it to, one paragraph to another, and to see if you have any unnecessary parts or gaps. Then revise as needed.

(Adapted from *The Right Handbook,* by Belanoff et al. in 1986, Boynton-Cook Publishers, Inc., Portsmouth, New Hampshire.)

To be sure your paragraphs flow logically one into the next, you should examine how the last sentence of each paragraph relates to the first sentence in the next.

Activity 2

Following is a long piece with no paragraph breaks. Read it and try to determine where the breaks should be. Then check to see if the last sentence in each paragraph relates to the first sentence in the next paragraph. When finished, discuss why you chose the paragraph breaks, and whether the paragraphs do flow smoothly one into the next.

Novels I Love

Four of my favorite novels are <u>Rebecca</u> by Daphne DuMaurier, Uncle Tom's Cabin by Harriet Beecher Stowe, <u>Jane Eyre</u> by Charlotte Bronte, and Nicholas and Alexandra by Robert K. Massie. <u>Rebecca</u> is a story of love, death, deception and intrigue among the wealthy in the early 1900s in England. A plain young woman of good character marries a wealthy widower and learns there are deep, dark secrets in his past. <u>Jane Eyre</u>, another mystery/romance novel, is about a plain young woman who was raised in an orphanage and then became a governess for the ward of a troubled, angry, and wealthy man. Mr. Rochester. She grew to love him, and was about to marry him when she learned of an impediment to their marriage, which made her flee, leaving him to grieve. Years of suffering followed for both of them, but the lovers found each other again in the end. <u>Uncle Tom's Cabin</u> is a tragic story about the hard life and sorrows of Uncle Tom, a noble and kind man of the enslaved black people in the American south. He is a lovable, self-sacrificing man who is ripped away from his wife and children, and sold to pay off gambling debts. He is later sold to the cruel, drunken Simon Legree, whose character is so hateful that his name has become commonly used to describe a selfish, cruel person. This historical novel, written in the 1800s, is so powerful that it caused millions to denounce slavery. Like <u>Uncle Tom's Cabin</u>, <u>Nicholas and Alexandra</u> is an historical novel. Set in Russia during the reign of the last Czar, it depicts the lives of Czar Nicholas II and his family amid the beginning of the Russian Revolution. Most of the novel is about the Czar and Czarina, their love for each other, their children, and the relatively private, oblivious lives they led in great wealth, while most of Russia suffered from poverty. The royal family did not avoid suffering. Their only son was born a hemophiliac, and his parents struggled to keep him alive. Their other six children were girls. An important player in their lives was the ill-reputed monk, Rasputin, on whom the Czar and especially the Czarina depended to cure their only son. I've read all four of these novels more than once, and I will probably read them again. It is such a pleasure to escape from daily pressures and worries, and return to Manderlay, Thornfield, the hovels of slaves in Louisiana, or the palaces of royals in St. Petersburg and Moscow.

Have a Writing Conference with Yourself

(adapted from N. Atwell, *In the Middle*)

Good writers spend a lot of time reading over and thinking about what they have written. Read your piece, then decide the weaknesses of the piece—the parts that need work—and its strengths—those parts that work so well that you want to do more with them. Last, ask yourself, "What is it I am trying to say here?" The following questions may help you to find and shape what you are trying to say.

Questions about Information

Do I have enough information?

What's the strongest or most exciting part and how can I build on it?

Have I shown (not told) by using examples? Is there anything confusing?

Have I told my thoughts and feelings at points where my readers will wonder?

Have I told where, when, and with whom this is happening?

Have I described the scene and people with enough detail that the reader can see it/them?

Does this piece need conversation? Did people talk? Have I directly quoted them?

Do I have too much information?

What parts aren't needed—don't add to my point or story?

Can I delete them?

What is this piece really about? Are some parts about something else? Can I cut them?

Do I have more than one story here? Which is the one I really want to tell?

Do I focus on just the important part(s) of the piece and delete the rest?

Is there too much conversation? Too many fussy details? Have I explained too much?

Questions about Leads, Conclusions, and Titles

Does my lead bring my reader right into my piece, into the main ideas or action?

Where does the piece really begin? Can I cut the first paragraph? What else can I cut?

Does my conclusion drop off and leave my reader wondering?

Does my conclusion go on and on?

How do I want my reader to feel at the end of the piece? Does my conclusion do that?

What do I want my reader to know at the end? Does my conclusion do that?

Does my title fit what the piece is about? Is it a "grabber?"

Would it make a reader want to read on?

Questions about Style

Have I used any word/words too much?

Are there too many unnecessary details?

Have I said something more than once?

Are any sentences too long and tangled? Too brief and choppy?

Have I paragraphed often enough to give my reader's eyes some breaks?

Have I broken the flow of my piece by paragraphing too often?

Is my information in order? Is this the sequence in which things happened?

Have I grouped together ideas related to each other?

Does the voice stay the same—first person participant (I did it) or third person observer (he or she did it)?

Does the verb tense stay the same (present/present continuous) (it's happening now) or past/past continuous (it happened before)?

Chapter Thirteen

EDITING

I have left editing toward the end of this book for some very important reasons. The main one is that it is very hard to achieve fluent writing if you are worrying about correctness or neatness. Let's go back over the writing process for a minute.

Writers must do three things—compose, revise and edit their work—three very different processes. **Composing** well entails writing pieces that people will enjoy reading because they are interesting, informative, funny, thought-provoking, sad, shocking, persuasive, entertaining, creative, touch the emotions, and are often memorable. Writers compose a first draft, then work on **revising** (making changes to improve it) it until they are satisfied that it is clear and that readers will enjoy it.

Editing is correcting mistakes. Too many people believe that writing well means producing a piece that teachers will approve of because it is written in a certain prescribed way, is neat, and has no errors. So they strive to avoid errors when they write, and to write in ways to please the teacher. Sadly, such pieces are usually hard to write, very dull and even confusing to read, because it's too hard to avoid errors and compose well if you are not yet a fluent writer. When you are a novice at writing, and try to do all three processes at once, you often do none of them well.

To understand why, you could compare learning to write with learning to speak your native language. You did a lot of experimenting as you acquired your native language, and you didn't worry about errors; you just focused on communicating. And so, as you spoke with family members, you learned to speak it fluently. Writing works this way, too. If you are a now fluent writer, you can start doing selective editing. If not, just use parts of this chapter and the next one for reference when you have a question. When you are ready for editing, I recommend that in addition to these two chapters, you obtain a grammar reference book, like *Rules of Thumb*, by Silverman et al. and the companion practice book, *Good Measures*.

Selective Editing

It is very hard to find and correct ALL of your writing errors when you begin to edit. To correct the most errors possible, you should begin to edit for the kinds of errors you make the most. For example, if you have 42 errors on a piece you've written—20 verb errors, 14 punctuation errors, 1 spelling error, 2 preposition errors, 1 word form error, 3 article errors, and 1 capitalization error—you'll get rid of MOST of your errors if you learn to correct the verb and punctuation errors: 34 out of 42!

Selective editing helps you to find your errors better. Think about classmates' papers that you have read. Have you noticed that it is pretty easy to find their errors? The reason is that you are reading their work for the first time, so you notice errors. But when you have written and revised your own work, and you know every word in it, you tend to read it much faster, and so you may not notice your errors.

Activity 1

To start the process of selective editing, take a piece of yours that has been corrected for errors by the teacher. Categorize the errors (see example below). Then count and add up the number of each of those types of errors in your piece, putting the number under each category, as in the following example.

Verbs	Wd. Order	Wd. Forms	Punc.	Spell.	Negs.	Art.	Preps.
20	0	2	9	1	2	3	2

Choose the one or two categories with the most errors. Write these down on the same sheet of paper (see example below), then further categorize your errors as "careless" or "real" based on whether you can correct them or not.

Careless errors are those you can correct without help, but that you made because you were concentrating on ideas and writing/composing well, which is good, and not on correctness. **Real errors** are ones you need help in correcting. If most of your errors are careless, you will be able to find and correct them, especially by focusing on just one or two of your most frequent errors.

For example, if you make most of your errors in verbs, you can go over your paper looking at your verbs. When you get used to editing for careless verb errors, you can add another type, like punctuation errors, as in the following.

ERRORS

VERBS		PUNCTUATION	
Careless	Real	Careless	Real

Activity 2

Now take 3 of your pieces that have not been corrected. On a separate sheet of paper, make a list like the one above, but with just one or two main categories. Correct the pieces yourself, but look for only those one or two types of errors. Keep a count of them on your list; then add up how many careless errors you made. Get someone to help you find and explain any real errors you made in those categories.

Do this for the other pieces you have written so far, even your freewrites. This practice will help you to get rid of most of your errors

Real Errors

Your real errors in each category are the ones you need help on. Your teacher will help you with them, and since there are not many, you will surely learn from them. When you can correct all or most of your errors in one category, go on to the next.

Editing for Punctuation Errors

One of the most common and most serious mistakes in writing is to forget to put periods at the end of sentences. A good way to find and correct these errors is to read your pieces from the end to the beginning. That is, put your two index fingers on the last two periods of your written piece. Then read what's between those two periods. If it is a phrase like, "For the rest of my life," you will know that it is not a sentence, but only part of it, or a fragment. If there are many lines without periods, there may be many sentences running together. These are called run-on sentences. So you must try to find the places where the sentence actually stops, and put periods there. If you keep editing from the last sentence to the first, you are more likely to find and correct fragments and run-on sentences. These rules may also help:

PERIODS are necessary to mark sentence endings, as in the following:

Everyone likes to be popular. Even shy people want others to notice and like them. However, the more outgoing a person is, the likelier he or she will be more popular.

COMMAS: separate items in a series and multiple adjectives; set off introductory phrases and clauses, and non-essential words, phrases and clauses. For example:

We had chicken, rice, peas, and salad for dinner. George is tall, dark, thin, and handsome.

When dinner was finished, everyone had coffee. Jack, on the other hand, is short and stout.

COLONS: precede lists; emphasize points; separate related sentences when the second explains the first; and introduce quotations. For example:

You need five ingredients: olive oil, garlic, parsley, basil, and tomatoes.

The bottom line was this: No one tried to help him.

As my dad used to say: "When in doubt, bail out."

SEMICOLONS: separate independent clauses that are closely related and word groups already divided by commas, as in:

He's so versatile: he's a computer whiz; he plays the piano; and he speaks four languages.

Is it a Sentence or a Fragment?

Along with editing from the last sentence to the first, you should know how to identify a subject and verb—the two components that make up a sentence. Here are some examples of sentences:

He knows the answer.

> **Subject: He**　　　　**Verb: knows**　　　　**Object: answer**

We agree.

> **Subject: We**　　　　**Verb: agree**

The bus just left.

> **Subject: bus**　　　　**Verb: left**

Questions are also sentences.

Have you seen Fran?

> **Subject: you**　　　　**Verb: have seen**　　　　**Object: Fran**

Where are they?

> **Subject: they**　　　　**Verb: are**

Commands are sentences with implied (you) subjects.

Be quiet!

> **Subject: (you)**　　　　**Verb: be quiet**

Don't do that!

> **Subject: (you)**　　　　**Verb: don't do**　　　　**Object: that**

Activity 3

Read the following sentences and determine the subject and the verb. N.B. A verb may have more than one word, as in "John (subj.) **must have left** (verb)

1. Peter has worked there for years.

2. Nobody understands.

3. What did they say?

4. Today is my birthday.

5. The children are learning how to read.

6. You shouldn't smoke.

7. She was taken to the hospital.

8. When he called, I was asleep.

9. They are getting married.

10. Your check has arrived.

11. Is that your wallet?

12. Sit down and don't say a word.

Activity 4

Edit the following piece for fragments (non-sentences) and run-on sentences by using the technique described before: i.e. read one sentence at a time from the last sentence back. Remember to read what's between periods to see if they are sentences, fragments, or run-ons. And keep in mind that a sentence is a complete thought with a subject and a verb, as in *"My tooth hurts,"* but not, *"When I was little,"* which is not a complete thought. A run-on is more than one sentence without a period after the first sentence, as in *"I took some aspirin, that helped a little."* And a fragment is not a sentence, as in *"The next day at noon."*

Her hair was long, thick and black, her face was beautiful, she looked like a young movie star, she was twenty seven when I was born. I was the second. Of eight children. And she took care of all of us. Which wasn't easy. Sometimes my brothers would be wrestling on the floor and practically killing each other, sometimes someone would have a bloody nose. Or a bleeding facial gash. And there would be crying and shouting, "He did it" "No I didn't, you big brat, you did it." She wouldn't get angry or yell, she'd just try to separate them, patch up cuts, or tend to bruises, she didn't panic.

But when my father came home. He'd go crazy. "Why do you have to give your mother such a hard time?" He would yell. "You know you're forbidden to fight in this house. Whether I'm here or not. That's the rule. For everyone in the house. Including all of you." And she'd say. "Dear, don't fuss, they'll behave better from now on, they promised me." "Now. Everyone wash your hands, let's all eat dinner, it's getting cold." Then he would calm down. After we all had assembled at the table. My father would say grace, and my mother would smile. And wink at us. Because by then, my father and my brothers had forgotten the fight. And were busy eating.

She used to wink at us a lot. Especially when she was giving us secret permission. To do something that our father would not allow. It was usually something like staying out later than we should have, she would give us permission but swear us to secrecy, and we would have to plan what time we would sneak in. At that time. She would leave a door unlocked. So that we could slip in unnoticed. Unless by chance Dad woke up or suddenly appeared where we weren't expecting him. But even so. He always forgave her after getting mad, he couldn't stay mad at her for long.

Capitals, Underlining, & Quotations

Capitalizing: Capitalize the first word in every sentence, proper names of people, countries, towns, states, oceans, rivers, buildings; streets, roads, boulevards, highways, and anything else with a proper name); the names of the months, the days, and the planets; titles preceding names; and abbreviations of titles (e.g. Dr., Ms., Mr., Mrs., Prof.).

Underlining: Underline titles of books, magazines and newspapers.

Using Quotation Marks: Use quotation marks before and after direct quotations, and for titles of plays, songs, paintings, poems, short stories, articles, essays and chapters in books.

Editing for Spelling Errors

If you have spelling errors, list them in a section of a notebook, study them, and ask someone to test you. There is no other way to learn them. When in doubt, ask your teacher. If you work on a computer, use the spell checker. And as you read your books, try to photograph into your memory the spelling of new words, or say their spelling to yourself a few times without looking at the word. Read over the rules that follow, and consult them when necessary. But otherwise, don't worry about spelling for the time being. Worry about writing interesting stories!

Spelling Rules

1. "I" before "e", except after "c", and in some words that have the long "a" sound, as in these examples: believe, retrieve, niece

   Exceptions: conceive, receive, ceiling, neighbor, weigh, vein, reign, leisure, neither, science, either, height, seize, foreign, conscience

2. For one-syllable verbs ending in a vowel and a consonant, you must double the final consonant before adding -ed or -ing.

   hop hopped hopping rot rotted rotting tip tipped tipping
   N.B. In such words, the vowel is short.

3. For verbs ending in a consonant and "e", do not double the final consonant, but drop the "e", before adding -ed or -ing, as in hope/hoped/hoping and advise/advised/advising

   N.B. In such words, the end vowel is "long" (i.e. like the alphabet sound).

4. For verbs ending in a consonant and "y", you form the past by dropping the "y" and adding "ied" as in cry/cried, rely/relied, hurry/hurried, and carry/carried.

5. For verbs ending in a vowel and "y", add "ed" as in play/played and toy/toyed.

6. For two-syllable verbs that stress the second syllable and end in a vowel and consonant, double the final consonant before -ed and -ing, as in defer/deferred/deferring,

   extol/extolled/extolling, and expel/expelled/expelling.

   If the same kind of verb has the accent on the first syllable, just add -ed or -ing, as in exit/exited/exiting, cancel/canceled/canceling, and focus/focused/focusing.

7. For nouns that end in "y", form the plural by dropping the "y" and adding "ies" as in city/cities, fly/flies, penny/pennies.

8. Learn the differences between: they're/their/there; you're/your; we're/were; no one/none; all ready/already; though/through; any subject "ain't."

Articles and Prepositions

Articles

The articles in English are "the", "an" and "a". "An" and "a" are easy to use. They both refer to a singular, unspecified item. For example, "a cup of coffee" or "an apple". "A" is used with words beginning with consonants, or vowels pronounced as consonants (e.g. the "u" in "used" /yuzd/, "a used car"). "An" is used before vowels or silent consonants followed by vowels (e.g. an honest woman). "The" refers to a specific item, e.g. I want the book I lent you last week. It is not used with general items, as in many languages. For example, we do not say, "I like the sugar." We do say, "Pass me the sugar" if it's a specific bowl of sugar that we have in mind. This is true of plurals as well as singulars. For example, we do not say "The people are funny" if we are speaking about people in general. But we do say "I like the people in my class."

Prepositions

Among the most common, yet problematic, prepositions in English are at, in, and on.

IN generally means "inside"; and "within" when referring to time.

AT generally indicates a location or a specific time.

ON generally indicates a surface, a specific day, or date.

Then there are hundreds of verb/preposition combinations, and these you simply have to learn one by one, e.g. think about, leave for, tire of, get married to, insist on, depend on, etc. Again, when in doubt, use a dictionary or ask the teacher for the correct preposition.

Negatives

In Standard Written English, we do not use double negatives. If we have a negative verb, for example, there is no other negative word in the sentence. E.g. *He didn't have any enemies. I don't believe anything she said. We haven't done anything.*

If we have a negated object, then the verb cannot be negative. E.g. *He had no enemies. She said nothing. We saw no one there.*

If we have a negative adverb, like "never," the verb in the sentence must be positive. E.g. *I have never met anyone like her.* or *I haven't ever met anyone like her.*

Remember the correct negative verb forms, too. We say "don't" with "I, you, we, they, and combinations like "You and I" and "John and Mary." E.g. *They don't speak English.* We say "doesn't" only with singular, 3rd person subjects like "he, she, it, Mary, a thing," etc. For example, *"He doesn't understand." "She doesn't like cats." "The train doesn't stop here." "It doesn't matter."*

Other/Others/Another

We use the word "other" before **plural** nouns: e.g. *other people, other days, other books, other ideas.* E.g. *The meeting was about other matters, not the parade.*

We use the word "another" before singular nouns: e.g. *another day, another piece of pie, another job, another place.* E.g. *You should look for another job.*

We use the word "others" as a plural pronoun, and another as a singular pronoun. E.g. *Some people didn't like the movie, but others said it was great. This was a great cup of coffee. May I please have another?*

To, Too, Two

"Too" means also or too much; "two" means 2; and "to" is for everything else.

He and I, We and They, You and I, She and I

Today it is common to hear sentences like, "Him and me are best friends," "Us and them are going on vacation," "You and me should go into business," "Her and me are going steady," or "Me and her are going steady."

What's wrong with these sentences? Object pronouns are in the subject position. The correct sentences would be, "He and I are best friends," "We and they are going on vacation," "You and I should go into business," "She and I are going steady."

We wouldn't say, "Him is my friend," "Me is going to the store," "Her should study," "Us" or "Them are going on vacation." So why would we combine those object pronouns as subjects?

Another rule: Don't put "I" before others. E.g. You and I should go into business." Not "I and you should go into business."

Chapter Fourteen

MORE EDITING FOR
VERB ERRORS

This chapter is for reference, to consult when/if you are ready to edit for verb errors.

PRESENT TENSE is used for **generalities, pronouncements** and **habits.**

    e.g.   I/you/we/they *KNOW/DON'T KNOW* how to dance.

                 He/she/it *KNOWS/DOESN'T KNOW* how to dance.

    e.g.   We *don't like it.* I *quit.* He *doesn't talk* a lot.

PRESENT CONTINUOUS TENSE is used for **present actions** and **future plans.**

    e.g.   I *AM/AM NOT EATING* because I feel sick just now.

                 He/she/it *IS/ISN'T* or *IS NOT LISTENING* to us.

                 You/we/they *ARE/AREN'T* going to the party.

    e.g.   It's *raining.* We're *getting married* in July.

PRESENT PERFECT TENSE is for **actions that started in the past and continue;** ones that have just occurred, and questions with indefinite past time.

    e.g.   I/you/we/they *HAVE/HAVEN'T WORKED* for the past two months.

             He/she/it *HAS/HASN'T WORKED* for the past two months.

    e.g.   We've always *lived* here. John *has arrived. Has* it *started?*

Some past participles do not end in -ed. Consult list (next page) for irregulars.

PRESENT PERFECT CONTINUOUS TENSE is used for recent sustained time/duration.

    e.g.   I/you/we/they *HAVE/HAVEN'T BEEN WAITING* for the results.

             He/she/it *HAS/HASN'T BEEN FEELING* well.

    e.g.   I*'ve been waiting* for an hour. It*'s been raining* all day.

Irregular Past Participles

be – been	freeze – frozen	see – seen
beat – beaten	get – gotten	seek – sought
become – become	give – given	sell – sold
begin – begun	go – gone	send – sent
bend – bent	grow – grown	set – set
bet – bet	hang – hung	shake – shaken
bite – bitten	hear – heard	shoot – shot
bleed – bled	hide – hidden	show – shown
break – broken	hit – hit	shut – shut
bring – brought	hold – held	sing – sung
build – built	hurt – hurt	sit – sat
buy – bought	keep – kept	sleep – slept
catch – caught	know – known	speak – spoken
choose – chosen	lay – laid	spend – spent

come – come	lead – led	spread – spread
cost – cost	leave – left	stand – stood
cut – cut	lend – lent	steal – stolen
dig – dug	let – let	strike – stricken
do – done	lie – lain	sweep – swept
draw – drawn	light – lit	take – taken
drink - drunk	lose – lost	teach – taught
drive – driven	make – made	tear – torn
eat – eaten	mean – meant	tell – told
fall – fallen	meet – met	think – thought
feed – fed	pay – paid	throw – thrown
feel – felt	put – put	understand – understood
fight – fought	quit – quit	wear – worn
find – found	read – read	weep –wept
fly – flown	ride – ridden	win – won
fit – fit	ring – rung	wind – wound
flee – fled	rise – risen	withdraw – withdrawn
forget – forgotten	run – run	withhold – withheld
forgive – forgiven	say – said	write – written

PAST TENSE is used for completed actions, past generalities, and present wishes. There are many irregular past tense forms; consult the following list.

e.g.   (Any subject) *WORKED/DIDN'T WORK* (except irregulars, below)

e.g.   He *arrived* late. We *didn't know* her. I wish I *had* three wishes.

be – was/were	grind – ground	see – saw
beat – beat	grow – grown	seek – sought
become – became	hang – hung	sell – sold
begin – began	have – had	sing – sang
bet – bet	hear – heard	sink – sank
bite – bit	hide – hid	sit – sat
bleed – bled	hit – hit	sleep – slept
blow – blew	hold – held	slide – slid
break – broke	hurt – hurt	speak – spoke

bring – brought	keep – kept	spend – spent
build – built	know – knew	spread – spread
catch – caught	lay – laid	stand – stood
choose – chose	lead – led	steal – stole
come – came	leave – left	strike – struck
cost – cost	lend – lent	swear – swore
do – did	let – let	take – took
draw – drew	lie – lay	teach – taught
drink – drank	light – lit	tear – tore
drive – drove	lose – lost	tell – told
eat – ate	make – made	think – thought
fall – fell	mean – meant	throw – threw
feed – fed	meet – met	understand – understood
feel – felt	pay – paid	wake – woke
fight – fought	put – put	wear – wore
find – found	quit – quit	weep – wept
forget – forgot	read – read	wind – wound
freeze – froze	ride – rode	withdraw – withdrew
freeze – froze	ring – rang	withhold – withheld
get – got	rise – rose	withstand – withstood
give – gave	run – ran	wring – wrung
go – went	say – said	write – wrote

PAST CONTINUOUS TENSE is used for an activity in progress in the past;

e.g. I/he/she/it *WAS/WASN'T WAITING* for two hours for that doctor. You/we/they *WERE/WEREN'T WAITING* for only 15 minutes.

e.g. *I was sleeping* when you called.

PAST PERFECT TENSE is used for past actions completed prior to other past actions, especially to denote different time periods. It is also used for wishes for the past.

e.g. Any subject *HAD/HADN'T WORKED* there for a long time before retiring.

e.g.   By the time you called, I *had* already *left*.

e.g.   I wish I *had gotten* an "A" instead of a "C" in that course.

PAST PERFECT CONTINUOUS TENSE is used for past continuous actions interrupted by another past action.

e.g.   Any subject HAD/HADN'T BEEN WORKING long when the fire broke out.

e.g.   By the time you arrived, I *had* already *been working* for seven hours.

FUTURE TENSE is used for the future and for refusals and polite requests.

e.g.   I/you/he/she/it/we/they *WILL/WON'T LEAVE* until next month.

e.g.   You *will be* 25 soon. I *won't do* it. *Will* you *help* me?

FUTURE CONTINUOUS TENSE is used for future events occurring at a certain time;

e.g.   I/you/she/he/it/we/they *WILL/WON'T BE GOING*.

e.g.   It *will be snowing* this time next month.

FUTURE PERFECT TENSE is used for actions that will be completed in the future;

e.g.   I/you/she/he/it/we/they *WILL/WON'T HAVE ARRIVED*.

e.g.   By the year 2010, I *will have worked* for 30 years.

MODALS indicate meaning, rather than time or tense. They include the words *shall, should, will, would, may, might, must, ought to, have to, can,* and *could.*

should/ought to/have to/must—indicate obligation or likelihood, from slight to strong (l to r).

can and *could* indicate ability, possibility, permission, or requests

may and *might* indicate possibility, permission, or polite requests

will/would—indicate intention, promise, refusal (with no)

shall—indicates a suggestion. It used to be the I/we form for "will."

Examples: *You ought to stop smoking. If you get sick, you'll have to stop.*

Mom said I could have a party. Can you come?

May I please have some pie? He said he might study law.

I will be there; I promise. Will you marry me? I will.

Shall we dance? Shall I sing a song for you?

N.B. We use modals with the perfect "have" and the past participle to put them in past tense. But with "must", the meaning changes in the past: "must have" means "probably did". Also, be careful to spell the contracted forms correctly. People say "should of", "could of", and "must of" for the abbreviated "should've", "could've", "must've". Don't spell them with "of".

Examples: *You failed? You should have studied harder.*

I could have passed with a little more effort.

Mary may have left already.

She must have left; her car is gone.

114

IF/RESULT SENTENCES are constructed as follows:

For the future: If I *see* him, I *will invite* him. (present + future)

For the present: If I *saw* him, I *would invite* him. (past + conditional)

For the past: If I *had seen* him, I *would have invited* him. (past perfect + conditional perfect)

Volition

If someone wants another person to do something, we generally use the **infinitive, "to _____ ."** And we use the **object pronouns** (me, you, him, her, us, them) as subjects of what is being asked to be done. For example:

I want *John/him to mow* the lawn.

He ordered *us to clean* the room.

He told *me to go* jump in the lake.

I warned *them not to drink and drive.*

I urged *him not to smoke.*

He begged *us to lend* him the money.

We invited *them to go* dancing.

My mother asked *me to do* the laundry.

They ordered *us to leave.*

They forced *him to swallow* the medicine.

My teacher urged *me to study* harder.

I want her to tell the truth.

I need you to be there early.

She commanded *us to stand* at attention.

After the verb "wish" and the expression "If only," we use the past for the present, and the past perfect for the past. E.g. *I wish I had* a lot of money. He *wishes he had been* there. They *wish we had told* them the truth. I'd buy that car right now, *if only I had* the money! I got a "D" on the final; *if only I had studied* harder!

Prefer, Request, Insist, Demand

These verbs are followed by "that," the person, and the base form (i.e. no "to" or endings). For example:

I prefer *that you sit* here.　　　　　He requested *that you sit* here.

They insist *that you sit* here.　　　　We demand *that you sit* here.

Reported Speech

To report direct speech, put what you're reporting back a tense, and change the pronouns as needed. For example:

He said, "I don't understand."—He said that *he didn't understand.*

I said, "We will be there."—I said we would be there.

You said, "I haven't finished."—You said *you hadn't finished.*

Reported Commands

To report commands, just use the infinitive. For example:

He ordered the children, "Keep quiet."　He ordered the children *to keep* quiet.

I shouted to Jim, "Watch out."　　　　I shouted to Jim *to watch out.*

They said to me, "Wait there."　　　　They told me *to wait* there.

We said to her, "Be careful."　　　　We told her *to be* careful.

"Don't be late," she cautioned us.　　She cautioned us not to be late.

Notice that when you report a command with "said," change the verb to "told."

"Don't do that," he said.   He *told* me *not to do* that.

"Be quiet, children" she said.   She *told* the children *to be* quiet.

The teacher said, "Pay attention."   The teacher told us to pay attention.

Active Voice vs. Passive Voice

Passive voice is formed with the verb "be" and the past participle. In active voice, the subject comes first. But to emphasize the object of an action, we can put it first:

Active	**Passive**
Someone has stolen my purse.	My purse has been stolen.
They took Thomas to the hospital.	Thomas *was taken* to the hospital.
They're going to fire Jeanette.	Jeanette is going to be fired.

N.B. A few verbs are always passive.

e.g. I *was born* in 1980. We *are supposed* to be there at 7.

Activity: Try your verb know-how, but don't fret if you get some wrong. Verbs take time to learn! Just refer to this chapter when necessary.

1. He (not/understand) _____ anything you said.

2. I speak English, but I (not/speak) _____ it well.

3. My sister just (have) _____ an operation.

4. Where (you/go) _____ last night?

5. We (have) _____ lunch together tomorrow.

6. (it/rain) _____ right now?

7. (John/know) _____ how to swim?

8. I (take) _____ some aspirin hours ago, but it (not/help) _____ .

9. (you/believe) _____ in ghosts?

10. I (work) _____ since early this morning.

11. How long (it/usually/take) _____ to get to the beach?

12. She told the children (not/make) _____ a mess.

13. What (you/do) _____ if (you/have) _____ an accident?

14. My son (be) _____ going to college next fall.

15. (you/see) _____ Mary anywhere lately?

16. I (live) _____ in this town since I (born) _____ .

17. They (call) _____ you, but you (be) _____ asleep.

18. He said he (know) _____ the answer, but he (not) _____ .

19. Max (bark) _____ so much last night that I (can/not) _____ sleep.

20. Nobody (like) _____ to be (criticize) _____ .

Chapter Fifteen

PUBLISHING YOUR WRITING

Publishing, or making our writing public, is what we can do when we have written a piece that we want to share with others. It is writing that we have worked on, revised and edited with an audience in mind. We can "publish" our writing by simply sharing our work with friends or family. Or we can look for a way to publish a book or a piece in a newspaper, magazine, anthology, or other publication.

You should illustrate, cover, and bind your 10,000 word projects, then share them with other classmates, other classes, family and friends. You could also send your work or a piece of it to be reviewed for publication in college publications or in other publications.

Preparing Your Book

Typing the Manuscript

It is best, as I said before, if you write your book on a word processor. This makes revising extremely easy. Typing is the second most preferable form, because it is far more readable than handwriting. But it is very hard to revise typewritten pieces. The least preferable form is writing by hand, but if you must do so, remember to write on one side of the page only, use erasable pens, write on every other line of the paper, and have scissors and transparent tape available so that you may move or remove pieces of text.

Illustrating the Manuscript

You might want to illustrate your pieces as they write, or do it at the end. You could have large drawings or pictures on separate pages in the text. You could put your illustrations on the left or right side of the page with the text on the other side, or you could make spaces within the text and put illustrations there.

There are various ways you may illustrate your text: with photographs, drawings, charts, maps, or computer graphics. You may take pictures from magazines, but you must acknowledge your sources. Readers usually like visual aids: they provide more information and a kind of intellectual relief as well. That is why magazines and newspapers use them, and many authors of books do so as well. If you are using a word processing program, use one that has a graphics package that you may use.

Titles

You should have titles for your pieces, ones that will draw people in and tempt them to read them. We call these "catchy" titles. Writers use popular phrases, song titles, single words, questions, exclamations, adjectives, names, quotes and other kinds of titles to entice readers.

Think about newspaper headlines, for example. They are brief, almost telegraphic, with few verbs, articles or inflections, yet they convey a good deal of information. Sometimes they are quotes or parts of quotes; other times they are just one word that says a lot, like "War!"

Organize Your Book, Anthology, or Magazine

Your book or magazine should have a cover, a hard one if possible. And on the cover should be the title of the book, in the center of the page and the center of the line, and in large letters. Then a little below it should be your name. Then your first page should also have the title, the author's name, the name of your class and school, and the year of publication.

On the next page you may dedicate the book to someone, giving his/her name, and perhaps a few words about why you are dedicating the book to that person. If necessary, you may write a foreword on the following page, if there is material you need to explain to the reader before s/he reads the book. The next page will be your table of contents, listing the chapters by number and name, and putting the page numbers of the chapter to the right. Then will come your text. Your text pages should be numbered at the bottom center, beginning with Arabic number 1. Make sure to start each chapter on a separate right-side page, number each chapter, and write the title of the chapter centered and in larger letters than the text itself.

Consult this book for examples. See how I wrote a title page, a table of contents with page numbers of chapter titles on it, and a dedication. Also notice how each chapter begins on a new page and on the right hand side, and the numbers at the bottom and center of each page.

Activity 1

Go back over any pieces you have written so far. If you haven't titled them, do so. Then ask your group members for their opinions of your titles.

Activity 2

Illustrate your pieces as you see fit. Autobiographies should include pictures or sketches, and perhaps a time line. Feature articles should include pictures, graphs, maps, or other graphics that will enhance the pieces. Fictional pieces can include sketches of scenes and characters.

Activity 3

Cover your project(s) with durable covering. Then bind it in some way that will be relatively permanent. You could have your work bound at a copying place, or bind it yourself.

Share and Celebrate

During the last week of class, your teacher may set aside time for you to display the books you have written, and for the rest of the class and invited guests to read and discuss them. I usually have refreshments and invite students and some of my colleagues to come in, have something to eat and drink, and sit down and enjoy reading one of the "books" on display.

Save Your "Book"

Be sure to save your book, because it will give you a lot of pride and satisfaction, will delight your family and friends, and may some day show a future teacher or employer what you can do as a writer. Finally, **Congratulations! You are now a published author!**

Bibliography

Atwell, Nancie (1998). *In the Middle,* 2nd Ed. Portsmouth, NH: Heinemann.

Belanoff, Pat, Betsy Rorschach & Mia Oberlink (1986). *The Right Handbook.* Portsmouth, NH: Boynton Cook.

Bronte, Charlotte (1987). *Jane Eyre.* New York: Bantam Books. (Original work published 1847)

Calkins, Lucy McCormick (2001). *The Art of Teaching Writing.* Portsmouth, NH: Heinemann.

DuMaurier, Daphne (2001). *Rebecca.* New York: Perennial. (Original published in 1938)

Elbow, Peter (1973). *Writing Without Teachers.* New York: Oxford University Press.

Fletcher, Ralph & Joann Portalupi (1998). *Craft Lessons.* Portland, ME: Stenhouse Publishers.

Hubert, Karen M. (1976). *Teaching and Writing Popular Fiction: Horror, Adventure, Mystery, and Romance.* New York: Teachers & Writers Collaborative.

Krashen, Stephen M. (2004). *The Power of Reading,* 2nd edition. Libraries Unlimited, Inc.

Ledoux, Denis (1993). *Turning Memories into Memoirs: A Handbook for Writing Life Stories.* Lisbon Falls, Maine: Soleil Press.

Massie, Robert K. (1967). *Nicholas and Alexandra.* New York: Dell Publishing

Mayher, John, Nancy Lester & Gordon Pradl (1983). *Learning to Write/Writing to Learn.* Portsmouth, NH: Boynton/Cook-Heinemann.

Portalupi, Joann & Ralph Fletcher (2001). *Non Fiction Craft Lessons.* Portland, ME: Stenhouse Publishers.

Rule, Rebecca & Susan Wheeler (1993). *Creating the Story.* Portsmouth, NH: Heinemann.

Silverman, Jay, Elaine Hughes & Diana Roberts Wienbroer (1999). *Good Measures: A Practice Book to Accompany Rules of Thumb,* 4th edition. Boston: McGraw-Hill.

Stowe, Harriet Beecher (1995). *Uncle Tom's Cabin.* Wordsworth American Library. (Original work published 1852)

Willis, Meredith Sue (1984). *Personal Fiction Writing: A guide to writing from real life.* New York: Teachers & Writers Collaborative.